FIRE ON
THE ALTAR

JOEL & JENNIFER CHUKS-NWOKIKE

FIRE ON THE ALTAR

by Joel & Jennifer Chuks-Nwokike

Paperback ISBN 978-0-578-16051-1

Published by Saving The Nations Ministries Int'l (USA)

DEDICATION

We would like to dedicate this book to our Lord Jesus Christ, who gave his life so that we could experience the person of God. Through the finished work of our Lord Jesus Christ, we can come boldly into the presence of God and experience the refiners fire of God.

ENDORSEMENTS

Larry and I have walked with Joel and Jennifer Chuks for over 8 years. The one thing we know is, Joel's heart is for the broken and lost. From the streets to the church, their lives reflect the gospels of Christ. I believe anyone who reads this book will be encouraged, charged up an fired up to take the Gospel into the world in these last days. This book will set your hearts ablaze once again.

- *Angela Greenig Ministries*

Easy to read, personal and well written with a message much more than surface deep… "One of the best books we have ever used". This book will help change many lives.
- *Daniel Rozen, Senior Pastor Living Stone Ministry Israel*

I appreciate all those who carry a righteousness message and whose desire is to call the church up higher to live a holy life set fully upon the Lord and moving in His presence and power to the glory of Jesus throughout the world. This book is not for the casual reader, or the easily offended. It is a sober call to reflection upon scripture and the intent of God for His people in the earth.

- *Robert Hotchkin*
  XP Ministries

I love my Brother, Joel - and his wife, Jennifer. I enjoy the way he lives his life, his focus on Christ Jesus, and how his speech goes right to the mark. There is joy in him, yet there is no fooling around with the truth of the Kingdom. I am into this book, and look forward to every page. There are gems in here that already have caused me to ponder what God might have me adjust in my own life. For me, that is key to my delight in what I give access to in my heart. May God bless your reading and your praying truth into your spirit - you will find the Word of God permeating every page. Enter open, leave blessed.

- Brad Gill, President
Christian Cable Ministries

A Relevant Case Study for every scriptural based servant of God with a determination to encounter God's abiding Glory Continuously. A blessing and must read.

-Dr Emmanuel Ziga, President
Grace For All Nations Ministries

CONTENTS

Introduction

"The fire on the altar shall be kept burning on it. It shall not go out, but the priest shall burn wood on it every morning; and he shall lay out the burnt offering on it, and offer up in smoke the fat portions of the peace offerings on it. Fire shall be kept burning continually on the altar; it is not to go out." *(Leviticus 6:12-13)*

"And Abraham took the wood of the burnt offering, and laid it upon Isaac his son; and he took the fire in his hand, and a knife; and they went both of them together." *(Genesis 22:6)*

Following the resurrection of Jesus Christ, those who have put their faith and trust in him as their Savior are called to make a spiritual altar and offer themselves upon it (Romans 12:1, 2). Just like in the Old Testament, whatever is offered on the altar is to be burned. However, this spiritual fire is the fire that God lights up himself. You are to burn the wood every morning by constantly presenting your life to him, sacrificing anything that will cause your flesh to elevate itself above your spirit, which is burning before God. The problem is some of us have allowed our flesh to stand in the way of our burning for God. It is God's heartfelt desire that this altar you have become be a purified and sanctified place where you encounter God. In the Old Testament men built and set up an altar wherever and whenever they encountered God. In Genesis 28, Jacob encountered God and set up an altar. He named it Bethel which means a place or house of God. Then years later God commanded him to return to Bethel, which is where he met his brother Esau. Prior to this meeting, Jacob got alone with God and spent time in prayer where he wrestled with God throughout the night. Prayer is a means of encounter, when you are praying you are burning the wood on the altar that keeps the fire burning. Other well-known men in the Bible built altars including Abraham, Moses, Joshua, and David.

The book of Mark records how, when Jesus was on the mount of transfiguration, Peter, James and John wanted to build an altar for him as well as Moses and Elijah. Once again, we see that altars were built following an encounter with God. However, Jesus did not endorse the idea, instead taking them back down the mountain he told them not to reveal what happened until after the resurrection.

The purpose of this book is to challenge us to never allow the fire inside of us to go out. Jesus Christ said in Revelation 3:15, 16 that they were not cold or hot but lukewarm. He then went on to say that this so angered him that he was going to spew them out of his mouth; in other words they made Jesus want to throw up. It is also significant that this is the only church of the seven listed that Jesus had nothing good to say about.

He also warned them if they didn't repent he would remove their candlestick, or influence in the community. The candlestick was a picture of the candlestick in the tabernacle and then later, the temple. It was never supposed to go out.

God is raising up a burning generation. They no longer want religion; they are tired of church programs that are nothing more than well-crafted productions to appeal to the flesh in an attempt to entice the world to come in. Instead this burning generation is consumed with seeing a manifestation of the presence of God. There is a shift brewing in the air as we are heading towards a change in the seasons where the church is preparing to arise and take their place and become a habitation of God. We have been promised the former rain and the latter rain, and the storm clouds are now on the horizon, but we have to let the fire burn in us with an intensity that is so great it becomes a roaring inferno that will consume us with the presence of God.

If that is what your heart is crying out for I would encourage you to continue reading, but if you just want to settle for religion, I would like to suggest that you think twice about Jesus Christ willingly and gladly sacrificing his life on the altar of God to enable you to have access into the holy place where you can become a heavenly manifestation of the kingdom of God here on earth.

1

EYES TO SEE & EARS TO HEAR

"So we fix our eyes not on what is seen, but on what is unseen. For what is seen is temporary, but what is unseen is eternal." *(II Corinthians 4:18)*

One of the biggest atrocities occurring in the church today is the inability or unwillingness of believers to utilize their spiritual eyes and ears. Jesus spoke many times about spiritual blindness and deafness (Matthew 15:14; 23:24 23:26). He referred to the religious leaders as being not only blind, but also leading other blind people astray (John 9:40-41). What would this look like in our churches today? Picture educated men and women sitting down in public meetings with their clerical collars or name tags displaying their title while brandishing their credentials and seminary degrees and pastoring hundreds and thousands of people. Now imagine Jesus showing up and telling them that far from being enlightened with great spiritual truths, they are nothing more than the blind leading the blind. These religious types are rooted in pride, which is the biggest barrier to receiving spiritual sight. Jesus rebuked the Pharisees in Matthew 23:17, referring to them as "Blind Fools."

Before Saul was transformed by Jesus into Paul, the apostle to the gentiles, the spirit of God knocked him off his high horse by a blinding light that was so bright that he laid there for days. Prior to his Damascus experience, in Saul's own eyes, he believed he was right and was walking in pride. He was so convinced he was right in his way of serving God that he went about killing, murdering, and torturing Christians, believing that was his mission. He was convinced that he was in the perfect will of God.

When a person is spiritually blind, they can be told something a million times and still not "get it." For example, when a person is in an abusive relationship and their family desperately tries to get them out of it, many time the person doesn't "see" anything wrong with the relationship and remain in it. The end result is often violence and sometimes even murder, and their future is stolen from them because they couldn't "see" anything wrong. Drug addicts are slowly killing themselves by injecting poison into their veins and you try over and over again to convince them that they should stop, but they can't see what is happening to them because the demon tells them there's nothing wrong with what they're doing, and besides, they're not hurting anybody else. Their eyes have been blinded to the truth, causing them to perceive a lie.

We also see spiritual blindness in unbelievers who look at themselves in the mirror and believe things are going along perfectly fine in their life. They think they don't need God, all they need is their sphere of influence, or right connection, or to have enough money in their bank accounts. The bible warns that their eyes have been blinded by Satan himself. "The god of this age has blinded the minds of unbelievers, so that they cannot see the light of the gospel of the glory of Christ, who is the image of God." (II Corinthians 4:4)

If you ask a spiritually blind person where they will spend eternity, they will often tell you they don't believe in heaven or hell; God or Satan. After all, they reason, why would a loving God send people to a burning hell? They will tell you that they are good people. They don't lie, cheat or steal, or hang out with those who do. They are perfectly right in their own eyes, but their eyes are blinded, and they are unable to see or perceive truth.

If your eyes were instantly opened to the spirit realm right now, you would see millions of angels and demons going about doing their business. We would see the invisible war going on in the heavenly realms above our heads. We would witness angels accompanying the children of God as they go about their daily lives. We would see them crossing the streets, guiding cars and airplanes, in churches and the homes of believers. You would also see demonic beings trying to entice people into sin. You might ask, "How is that possible?" Very easily. There are demonic spirits who attach themselves to instruments or items that are used as points of contact for invoking their assignments, which is always to lead people into sin, which eventually leads to death. They can be attached to your computer or phone (where the doors have been opened to the demonic realms through pornography, sexual perversion and vulgar music). Demons just lie in wait for any open opportunity they have been given. Once they are granted access, they bring seven stronger ones with them.

"Then it goes and takes along seven other spirits more evil than itself, and they go in and live there; and the last state of that man becomes worse than the first" (Luke 11:26 NLT). This brings a greater level of sin, which creates a rapid demise of the person's spirit, soul, and body. "For the wages of sin *is* death; but the gift of God *is* eternal life through Jesus Christ our Lord" (Romans 6:23 NKJV) They also lie and wait for believers to speak curse words or negative things over themselves so they can use their own words against them. For example, if a believer is constantly speaking death over themselves by saying things like, "I'm so sick, I don't know how much longer I'm going to make it," they are inviting sickness, death, and demonic activity into their physical body. "Death and life *are* in the power of the tongue: and they that love it shall eat the fruit thereof" (Proverbs 18:21 NKJV). We will look at this scripture further in the fourth chapter "The Power Of The Tongue." Our environments are controlled by our mouths. You are what you say. If you're constantly speaking death, negativity, and curses over your children or spouse such as, "They're so lazy and stupid, and will never amount to anything," then you are opening demonic doors over your environment and families and bringing curses upon your home.

"**Open my eyes that I may see wonderful things in your law.**" **(Psalm 119:18)**

"**Pray also that the eyes of your heart may be enlightened in order that you may know the hope to which he has called you, the riches of his glorious inheritance in the saints.**" **(Ephesians 1:18)**

The prophet Isaiah had a personal revelation from God on spiritual blindness. Isaiah's mandate from the Lord was very clear. "Go and tell this people: You are ever hearing, but never understanding; be ever seeing, but never perceiving." (Isaiah 6:9) There is a difference between seeing and perceiving. God was telling Isaiah that his charge was to try and awaken the people of Judah who had turned to idolatrous worship. They were in a political uproar, there was pandemonium in the political system in which Israel had chosen to follow after money and military might. Isaiah describes the demise as "And the daughter of Zion, is left as a booth in a vineyard, as a besieged city" (Isaiah 1:8). Israel had turned from their God and forgotten him. "The ox knows his owner, and the ass his master's crib, BUT ISRAEL DOES NOT KNOW, my people do not consider" (Isaiah 1:3).

Isaiah's name means "The Salvation of Yahweh." It was God's desire to first bring awareness to his people of their spiritual condition, but that wasn't his only intent. His intent was that they be saved and that could only happen when their eyes were opened. It's like the old song that says, "Amazing Grace, how sweet the sound that saved a wretch like me. I once was lost but not I'm found, WAS BLIND BUT NOW I SEE."

There's nothing more frustrating for a person with sight than trying to explain something they see to a blind person. It cannot be done, only experienced. God's desire is that his children walk in the supernatural realm of spiritual sight, understanding, knowing, and hearing. The whole purpose of having eyes to see and ears to hear is for one reason, REVELATION. If you can see and hear, you will KNOW. You have that inward knowledge that you're a child of God. The ability to hear and see helps us know what his calling is for us. (Ephesians 1:18)

Have you ever wondered what your purpose is in life? What were you made for? God's purpose and plan for your life is good and not intended to harm you. We were created in his image, for his purposes. Idolatry is the worship of an image or idea that takes the place of God in our lives. The church in Ephesus had turned their back on God and were worshipping idols. Paul's prayer for the people in Ephesus who were spiritually blind and worshipping idols was that their eyes would be opened so they could see that their allegiance was to the Greek goddess Artemis, whose brother was Apollyon and these demonic idols were made in their image.

Paul tells them he would "pray also that the eyes of your heart may be enlightened in order that you may know the hope to which he has called you, the riches of his glorious inheritance in the saints" (Ephesians 1:18). Paul understood that he couldn't open their eyes no matter how much he tried. He couldn't teach them to receive spiritual sight, he couldn't pump them up so much that they received spiritual sight, but he realized that the Holy Spirit was the only one who could remove the blinders and open their eyes. This was the same Saul who became Paul after his encounter with the Lord and his eyes were opened (Acts 9:1-19), now testifying what God had done for him.

"He that hath an ear, let him hear what the spirit says to the church." (Revelation 2:7)

Spiritual deafness also runs rampant in the pulpits, homes, lives and government of our nation. We live in a generation where knowledge and resources are instantly at our fingertips. We've replaced quietness and listening to the voice of our Father with reading and listening to everyone else's opinion but his. If we want to know something, rather than turn to the word of God, we search out what pop culture says or what the latest talk on social media is. The voice of reason does not come from the outward opinions of man, but from the inside. There is an inner voice which enables the spirit of man to connect with the Holy Spirit who is the spirit of truth. He will always lead and guide us into truth. (John 16:13)

It is possible to listen and not hear, or hear and still be deaf. Have you ever tried to explain something to a person over and over but they don't allow it to sink in? That's because they are not receiving what you are saying. For example, if I walk outside right now and tell the first person that I see that Jesus is coming soon, they may look at me and let it go in one ear and out the other and shrug it off as me just being crazy. But faith comes by hearing, and hearing by the word of God.

The ability to hear truth allows us to speak it even when the whole world is saying something different. Jesus says in John 12:49 that he only speaks what he hears his father saying.

Spiritual hearing allows us to hear the inward leading of the spirit of God and to obey. My sheep hear My voice, and I know them, and they follow Me. (John 10:27)

The Spirit clearly says that in the latter times some will abandon the faith and give heed deceiving spirits and things taught by demons. (I Timothy 4:1)

As I'm writing this, where I live, in Washington State, our legislation has just passed laws last week stating that it is now legal for a man and man to marry and it's also legal to use recreational marijuana. We have turned our worship from God to idols and the separation between the sheep and the goats is getting greater every day.

We need Isaiah's who will stand in the face of these abominations and call them what they are straight up with no sugar coating or compromising in the name of being politically correct.

Isaiah was a proven prophet, serving the Lord for 55 to 60 years under four different kings (Uzziah, Jotham, Ahaz, and Hezekiah).

One of the biggest fears of a false shepherd is a sheep who has eyes to see and ears to hear what the Spirit of The Lord is saying to his church. Jesus said "My sheep hear my voice and a stranger's voice they will not follow." True followers of Jesus Christ will stand against the false doctrines and seducing spirits that are being taught in our churches today. When a person truly sees with the eyes of the spirit and hears what the Holy Spirit is saying, they will not take heed to religious rituals and bondages. Just because something looks and sounds good, doesn't mean it has your best interest at heart. The only one who knows your beginning, ending, and all of the time in between is your creator, and he knows what is best for our lives. When we hear his voice and know his heart, we are in the safest place of all, in the palm of his hand. Wars and fatalities could be breaking out all around you, but it will not come near you when you're under his shadow. (Psalm 91)

A few years ago, my wife and I were each offered a very nice salary with all of our personal expenses paid, with one condition; that we forfeit the missions ministry that God had given us and work for a religious organization full-time, if we would just forfeit the vision we had from God and align with their vision and doctrines of men. We didn't even have to consider this because even though it looked great, and sounded good to our ears, there was no question in our hearts that we would never abort the vision God had given us. We could not be bought or sold no matter what the cost. We had been given a promise and a glimpse of our future in Christ through the eyes of the Spirit and we knew that this opportunity wasn't in that vision, so we graciously declined. The lesson here was that even though this offer sounded good to our ears, we knew inside that it was wrong for us.

2

STRANGE FIRE & ABOMINATION ON THE ALTAR

"And Nadab and Abihu, the sons of Aaron, took either of them his censer, and put fire therein, and put incense thereon, and offered strange fire before the LORD, which he commanded them not." *(Leviticus 10:1)*

"Ye shall offer no strange incense thereon, nor burnt sacrifice, nor meat offering; neither shall ye pour drink offering thereon. And Moses and Aaron went into the tabernacle of the congregation, and came out, and blessed the people: and the glory of the LORD appeared unto all the people. And there came a fire out from before the LORD, and consumed upon the altar the burnt offering and the fat: which when all the people saw, they shouted, and fell on their faces." *(Leviticus 9:23, 24)*

"And the LORD spake unto Aaron, saying, Do not drink wine nor strong drink, thou, nor thy sons with thee, when ye go into the tabernacle of the congregation, lest ye die: it shall be a statute forever throughout your generations: And that ye may put difference between holy and unholy, and between unclean and clean; And that ye may teach the children of Israel all the statutes which the LORD hath spoken unto them by the hand of Moses." *(Leviticus 10:8-11)*

The bible speaks very clearly about "strange Fire" being offered to the Lord by Aaron's sons Nadab and Abihu. Strange fire was considered to be something that the Lord had not commanded them to bring to him. Why had Aaron's sons decided to nonchalantly bring their offering to the Lord? The bible says that they were drunk while offering their incense on the altar. Perhaps their judgment was impaired, causing them to feel that it was ok to approach the mercy seat in such a manner. Maybe pride had slipped in and they wanted to "out do" or "one-up" their father's ministration. All we really know is that Aaron's sons had witnessed their father Aaron and Moses do mighty exploits for God in front of the whole nation of Israel to the point where all the people saw the glory of the Lord appear to ALL THE PEOPLE (Lev 9:23). The people were on their faces, shouting before God as they witnessed his glory after Moses and Aaron had ministered before him on the altar through sacrifices that the Lord commanded them to offer. Maybe Nadab and Abihu coveted the miracles their father was doing and thought they could do better. They had a sense of entitlement, which is running rampant in the church today.

This mentality is similar to a copycat anointing, where a person who doesn't have a personal revelation of the plan of God for their life witnesses God using another person in a visible way that is known to many people, and they say well, if he can do it than I can do it. Not necessarily, because if you're called to be the eyes but you're trying to be the mouth, then you're job is not being done properly and there is disorder. For example, a man has many graces and gifts, one of which is preaching. He does it with ease, and he loves to do it. He preaches at every opportunity, anytime and anyplace. For another person, on the other hand, preaching is more of a task than a joy, and they have to study and put a lot of effort into their messages.

Just because someone is doing something well doesn't mean we have to run out and copy what they do. That shows immaturity and a lack of self-assurance in the gifts of God. The sin of Nadab and Abihu was deadly and as a result of their negligence they perished in the house of God.

I am so thankful for the grace of Jesus Christ by which we have all been saved. I'm not writing this to point fingers or pass judgment but to learn valuable insight here for ministers and those who work on the altar in churches today. Actually, if ministry was handled by God in this manner today, most of us, would definitely be six feet under; but because of the grace of Jesus Christ we can approach his throne of grace boldly, but with reverence.

Aaron's sons did not have any reverence for the house of God or for their father. If they would have valued their father and the mantle that was placed upon his life, they would have waited for their due time and season in which they could minister before the Lord. Instead, they lacked training, discipline, humility and reverence and therefore their lives were taken by God himself. I believe if these boys would have served their father and worked in the temple learning the way of the Lord, their ending would have been quite different. After all, the bible says they were drunk while attempting to minister to the Lord. This is still happening in the pulpits of America and around the world every week where the Pastor or Evangelist got so drunk the night before that they couldn't stand up. Then they get up the next morning and put on their best suit and smile and call it good, hiding their sin and offering strange fire on the altar.

We have a training center in Washington state, and we have had hundreds of people come into the church with a willingness to learn and be discipled, and then within six months, after their gifting's start to develop and the anointing begins to brew in their lives, they become the most arrogant, haughty people who claim to be the only ones who can "hear" from God.

Time after time, these people end up falling away because we know that pride comes before a fall. The gifts and callings of God are not administered by us, but were given to men by the grace of Jesus Christ, and you and I do not dictate who is called as a minister or priest before the Lord, and who is called to be a Sunday school teacher. Most people see the person behind the pulpit and think that it is a glamorous life, and that there is something to gain from being in that position.

Sometimes, the minister is even worshipped and placed before the Lord in the hearts of men, which is the sin of idolatry, and that sin is not taken lightly before God. If you're under a Pastor, Prophet, Apostle, Evangelist or Teacher (and you should be under one spiritually), please do not allow satan to tell you that you can do their job better. This is the same trick that satan tried to use against God, and he was thrown out of heaven for it. In Isaiah 14:14 Lucifer says, "I will be ascend above the clouds, I will be like the Most High." WOW!

He wanted to be higher than God, which is not even possible. Satan was a wannabe from the very beginning. John 15:20 says that the servant is never greater than his master. I'm amazed at the number of people who tell me that they don't have to submit to anybody, or at the number of people who leave ministries because they become offended after the

Pastor gave them a warning about something that wasn't right spiritually in their life. We've lost the honor and integrity in the body of Christ and we are so easily offended. Lack of submission and obedience is a major problem today in the body of Christ.

The instructions on how to offer their incense before God were precise. God is detail oriented and he likes things done a certain way, in excellence. He had given strict instructions to Aaron on how the altar should be kept, all the way down to the instruments used for ministration.

And he shall take a censer full of burning coals of fire from off the altar before the LORD, and his hands full of sweet incense beaten small, and bring it within the veil: And he shall put the incense upon the fire before the LORD, that the cloud of the incense may cover the mercy seat that is upon the testimony, that he die not. (Lev 16:12)

God even warned that if the altar was not kept in this manner then the priest would die. It's amazing to me how many churches there are in our city and I often wonder how many of those churches were actually planted and placed there by God or were instead started by self-appointed ministers. Just because a person graduates from seminary school doesn't mean he is called by God. And just because a Sunday school teacher is put in a back room instead of the pulpit doesn't mean that they weren't called to be the pastor. Apostolic ministry is in no way glamorous, it's grueling work and takes a toll on a person physically, mentally and in every way. Anytime a person is crossing international and national borders, building up and planting, tearing down strongholds in the heavenly realms and reaching people out of deep darkness into the light of Jesus Christ, its serious business. Our mentor is one of the greatest Prophetesses in the Kingdom of God today and she has suffered for the Lord in ministry for over 26 years. During that time she has been persecuted, lied about, and stolen from. I have witnessed these things happen to her over and over again and her response is always the same: LOVE.

There's nothing glamorous about how The Apostle Paul often referred to his calling from God as slavery or as a prisoner of Jesus Christ? Listen ministers, our lives were predestined. The Father knew us before we were in our mother's womb and he has predestined us. This life we live is not by choice, but destiny. We are mandated to carry our cross and die to self daily. God has a plan and purpose for each one of our lives (Jeremiah 29:11) and it's up to us to find out what our purpose is.

There is an African proverb that says there are two great days in a person's life. The first is the day you're born and the second is the day you find out why you were born.

In I Samuel 15:13 King Saul was anointed King of

Israel and commanded by God to destroy all the false idols in the nation and all the inhabitants, including men, women and infants.

Saul didn't do what he was told to do, but chose to keep the spoils and didn't kill the evil King.

When his sin was found out, he proclaimed his innocence but Samuel the prophet knew he was lying. Samuel said the Lord told him that Saul disobeyed and had done evil in the eyes of the Lord. Saul continued to claim that he was innocent because he intended to give the best to the Lord. Samuel said that obedience is better than sacrifice and rebellion is as the sin as witchcraft and arrogance is as idolatry.

Witchcraft: is rebellion, which is a spirit. And idolatry is the spirit of arrogance unto the Lord.

This same witchcraft is alive and well in the church today. In our city, one of the largest churches is showing Harry Potter to the children in Sunday school and bringing in illusionists for entertainment purposes. This is witchcraft and it has no place in the lives of Christians. Today, Christians live for themselves and put God's purposes for their lives on the backburner. Then some Christians will give God partial obedience, which is the same thing as disobedience. They are engaged in manipulation in an attempt to accomplish their own wills here on the earth. They manipulate people through evil spirits.

In Leviticus 10:1-3, Aaron's sons died on the altar because they offered strange fire. Incense in the bible in Revelation represents prayers and in Isaiah 1:12-15 God says he detests the Sabbaths and convocations (modern day conferences. He does not receive their prayers).

Ministers stand on a stage behind a Holy Pulpit, full of unholy deeds and hearts. Their mouths are preaching, teaching, releasing revelation and enticing the people's itching ears. However, inside their hearts are ravaging wolves. Their thoughts are of how much money they will bring in that evening. Many times they are looking with lust at their leaders, desiring another woman or man besides their wives. The sons of Aaron were sleeping with women in the church and were drunkards (Leviticus 10:1-3). America, we need to wake up and realize that this is happening all around us and it is not exposed because of fear and intimidation.

America's introduction to Christian media has been men preaching in thousand dollar designer suits sitting on King's thrones while living off of other people's earnings. This was how the sons of Aaron were behaving and although it was unnoticed by the people, God saw everything that was occurring.

I wonder what the women his sons were sleeping with were told, or how they were manipulated into sleeping with them. Maybe they were told that "God" had spoken to these ministers and that God wanted them to be together. If this sounds familiar it is, because this is what people are being told in American churches today. "God said you need to give me $20,000." Oh really? Did God tell the giver that? Witchcraft and manipulation are being practiced in the church right in front of God and the whole world. The mercies of God are so great that we are able to stand under his grace while these things are going on.

We have witnessed instances in our city where a married woman comes to the Pastor and said, "God told me that you are my husband." Really? I wonder which god told you that, the god of your flesh and lust. We need to get this leaven out of our lives so that God can do what he wants to do in his church.

Going back to the sons of Eli, when I started reading their story in the book of I Samuel, it blew my mind when I learned about the lifestyle that they lived from the altar, but unfortunately we still see that lifestyle in the kingdom of God today. We see many Christians go from the pulpit to watching porn. There is no longer a fear of God among His people. Remember in the book of Acts when Ananias and Sapphira lied and dropped dead in the church. God hasn't changed, we are still serving that same God, and his is still holy and righteous and cannot behold iniquity.

The reason we allow sin in our churches is because we are playing games in the church. Settling for religion instead of the presence of God. When the Glory of God starts to fill our churches like on the day that Isaiah saw the Lord in chapter 6, then we will see this country turn back to God.

People of God, we need the presence of God in our churches. Imagine how powerful our churches would be if we to all contend for the presence of God; if we became like Moses and Paul. Moses asked God to "show me your Glory" and Paul says "that I might know him." Programs and events don't change lives, an encounter with God does. When we set the atmosphere to make it conducive for the presence of God to manifest itself in our churches, we will become the Mount Zion where deliverance takes place. Our prayer is that sinners will run to our churches in our city. We pray and believe to witness repentance on such a large scale that our churches are full and the clubs are emptied.

How is it there so many people in our churches addicted to porn, drugs, alcohol, prescription drugs, and other vices? This ought not to be so. The presence of God can destroy all of that; by reason of the anointing every yoke shall be broken, not by programs, events, sing five songs and give offerings. No, by reason of the anointing. When the anointing of God becomes prevalent in our churches, people will begin getting healed and set free without anyone praying for them.

A mere touch of the garment of Jesus Christ was healing people; the shadow of Peter and the handkerchief of Paul were healing the sick, why? The bible says God anointed Jesus Christ, It says ANOINTED Jesus Christ (Acts 10:38).

But when there so much sin in the camp it hinders the presence of God from being able to manifest itself in our mist. The Angel had to purify Isaiah before he could step into the fullness of the realm of the spirit. Isaiah 51 says that the hand of God is not shortened, neither is he deaf to hear us, but the problem is that sin has separated us from him. But wait a minute, this is the same sin that Jesus Christ conquered for us. How can we allow something that has already been defeated to continue to defeat us, I will talk more about this in another chapter. But we have been redeemed by the blood of the lamb; sin doesn't have power over us anymore, but we keep going back to our old lifestyle because we want to CONFORM instead of TRANSFORM.

3

PRIVATIZING THE FIRE

"My heart was hot within me, while I was musing the fire burned: then spake I with my tongue." *(Psalm 39:3)*

The world gets a little confused about the motive of the church, and generally I don't blame them. We preach a gospel that says "Store up treasure in heaven for yourself in heaven where thieves cannot come in and steal," yet we are storing up our treasures here on earth and not thinking about eternity. We are becoming worldlier; there is a reason why Jesus says in Mathew 6:33 "seek first the kingdom of God and everything will be added unto it," but we are busy pursuing the wealth of this world that is supposed to be an addition to us. The anointing and calling of God is not for personal gain, Jesus says "freely you receive and freely you give." (Matthew 10:8)

When God called me into the ministry in 1997, I told Him that I will not be paid by the ministry to work for God. Now I'm not against a pastor getting paid, that's just my personal covenant with God. I came from a very poor background, but my family was not always poor. There was a time when my Dad was a very successful pastor with about five churches under him in Africa. Things had turned around for him after my mom died and we became poverty stricken. Sometimes it was very difficult for us to find food to eat. Unlike in America, in Africa we didn't have food banks so if you didn't have food you just didn't have it. My Dad had seven kids with my mom and later he remarried and had a total of 12 kids. Imagine providing food for all of those kids. I grew up always wanting to be better and not having to suffer like my Dad. So when I started in the ministry all I had in my mind was having a comfortable life, so I was always conscious of making sure I had enough money to pay the bills for the ministry, and for my wife and son. It got to a point where God started speaking to me and reminding me about seeking his kingdom first, and that he would make sure that I don't lack. I noticed that whenever I was worrying about not having enough money to pay for the bills of the ministry we were struggling financially, and I was completely stressed out until I learned how to trust God. And this is what I said to God "I will not stress out about the ministry finances anymore. If you provide the money I will do it and if you don't we will just let it be. This helped me to trust God completely to provide for his work and also bless me and my family for laying down our lives for the kingdom's sake.

The greatest reward in the kingdom is the reward that comes from hearing Jesus Christ say, "Well done thou good and faithful servant." That's a word I want to hear when I'm done here on earth and appear before our master, Jesus Christ.

When you are in love with the things of this world it changes your motive from being pure to being wicked. This is why we become so wicked and preach the gospel of getting something from the people. But wait a minute, these people didn't call you, God did, he is the one you should go to and request that he take care of you. When you do this, God becomes the one that touches the heart of the people to give instead of you manipulating them. Sometimes we get to the point where we don't care about God touching people anymore in our services, people getting healed, saved and delivered. Instead, tithes and offerings becomes our main focus, and we are no longer sensitive to the spirit of God to know what he wants to do in a service.

I was meditating one day and saying God, please don't allow me to get to the point in life where I'm living in a $3 million house and driving the most expensive cars while there are people in my church that can only afford to pay $500 for their house or rent, or even food for their family. Do we really need those expensive houses, cars and jewelry? That's why the world is confused, because we are telling them that this world is not our home, yet we are busy building our kingdoms and empires here on earth. Whatever happened to helping the poor or hazarding our lives for the kingdom's sake? What happened to making sure that the sheep eat first before the Shepherd does? There are so many hirelings in the kingdom of God, and that's why Jesus says that the hireling cannot lay down his life for the sheep because he really doesn't love them, they are just a paycheck to him.

I heard a story one time about a pastor whose congregation bought a very expensive car for him. He told them to sell it and put the money back in the church fund to help the poor among his congregation. Glory to God, isn't that what happened in the days of the apostles? People were selling their properties and bringing the money in and distribution was made to people according to their needs.

Gehazi lost the transfer of the anointing from Elisha because he was more interested in the things of this world than the anointing and the fire of God. Imagine what Gehazi could have become, the level of anointing he would have had, and the lives he could have touched. There had to be a reason why God told Elisha to not accept the offering from Namaan. Gehazi lost his destiny, calling, and the precious presence of God; and not just that he was humiliated. The leprosy of Namaan came upon him and was removed out of the camp. He became unclean, he lost his abode. The same thing happened to Judas. He lost his place as an apostle simply because he loved money more than he loved his master. One time we had a revival meeting in Taholah, Washington, and while preparing for the meeting the Lord spoke to me and said "When you get there, do not take up an offering because most preachers that have gone there have taken so much money from them that the people are skeptical and I cannot really show forth my presence and love." It wasn't easy because at the time our ministry needed finances, but I have learned to obey God at any given time. So we went there to feed the people and share the love of Jesus Christ. Many people gave their lives to Jesus Christ and some got delivered. Our team and I were so excited to see the love of Jesus Christ flow. Then about five days later someone dropped a check for $7,000 in the offering basket. Thank God I obeyed. Do you think he would have provided that money for the ministry if we hadn't yielded to his voice? Probably not.

You can't pursue the heart of God and the things of this world at the same time; you have to give up one or the other. That's why we preach and lives are not changed. The anointing is no longer flowing in our church services because the motive has been changed from seeking the heart of God to seeking the hands of God. Are you using your position for personal gain, not just as a pastor but as a businessman, maybe in your workplace. Are you more interested in privatizing the gift for your own gain, or are you interested in using it for the glory of the giver of the gift. The apostles never used the anointing for their own good. Even Jesus himself was faced with situations where he could have shown his power to prove that he is the son of God, but rather he decided to do just the will of the father, when we bring ourselves under the will of the Father it will bring us into a place of humility, I pray that the heartbeat of God becomes your heartbeat.

4

POWER OF THE TONGUE

"Even so the tongue is a little member, and boasteth great things. Behold, how great a matter a little fire kindleth! And the tongue is a fire, a world of iniquity: so is the tongue among our members, that it defileth the whole body, and setteth on fire the course of nature; and it is set on fire of hell." *(James 3:5, 6)*

How can such a small thing have such a great impact on a person's life? How can one body part the size of a finger kill a person or give a person life? You see, the bible says that the power of life and death are in the tongue. We literally have the power to bring blessing or curses, life or death with the words we speak. When we speak, our words vibrate with the frequency of the heavenly realms. Light is a wave just like sound and sound comes from words. Science has proven that if you break down a light beam into individual molecules, it is a wave with its own frequency. We have creative ability with our words to speak and the heavens have to obey. It is a spiritual law put in place at the time of creation. In Genesis Chapter 1 we see that God created the whole universe, including man and animals, vegetation, the waters and sea, and the whole blueprint of man's existence using his mouth. The bible says that God spoke and SAID, let there be light (Genesis 1:3) .... And he said let there be firmament, and there was. But when it came to creating Adam, God got personally involved in the dirt and formed man. He conducted spiritual CPR through his mouth by breathing life into man and he became a living soul. So since the bible says that you and I are made in the image of God then we can speak and watch things being manifested through God's creative power right before our very eyes. Well, you may say that's nice but does that mean if I say I'm going to be a millionaire that a million dollars will manifest itself in my living room right now? While it is certainly possible, it depends on the level of authority you have with your mouth. I guarantee that if you tell yourself, "I'm poor and will never be rich" than you will have exactly that. After all, how does a single man of God named Elijah make it rain after a severe drought simply by making a statement with his mouth? "And Elijah said unto Ahab, Get thee up, eat and drink; for *there is* a sound of abundance of rain"

(1 Kings 18:41). Or how can a man whose body was completely wracked with cancer be healed at the command of a person who laid their hands on his body and commanded the cancer to leave. Even cancer has to bow to the voice of a believer of Jesus Christ. Did you know that you have more power in your mouth than the combined might of all the hordes of hell? You have the power to create and change your circumstances and destiny with the words you speak. I challenge you to begin speaking life over yourself and your family. You can easily start by saying things like "My family is blessed."

Whatever we put our hands to do prospers The LORD your God will then make you successful in everything you do. He will give you many children and numerous livestock, and he will cause your fields to produce abundant harvests, for the LORD will again delight in being good to you as he was to your ancestors. (Deuteronomy 30:9)

We receive promotions at school, work and in our community because we are the head and not the tail (Deuteronomy 28:13). We have everything that we need and will not lack in Jesus' name because my God supplies all my needs according to his riches in glory in Christ Jesus (Philippians 4:19). We are well and healthy, and in our mind, soul and body we are prospering in everything we do and touch in Jesus' name (3 John 1:2 NLT). I hope all is well with you and that you are as healthy in body as you are strong in spirit.

These examples are changes of declarations that,

when spoken with faith, will bring changes into your home, family and life through declaring the Word of God.

So many times we say things, especially from the pulpit that are not helpful. Since there is no longer a holy reverence for God in our churches, a minister will often stand in the pulpit and lie and exaggerate just to get the attention of the people. We tell many stories just to keep the people entertained because we think the word of God is not powerful enough, and in the process of telling those stories we say things that never happened. Don't we care that there is a God that knew the story you were telling before it happened, and that he knows you are exaggerating. We don't need to help God; he alone has all the power he needs to release a word that will change someone's life. We have lost the fear of God in our churches, homes and schools, and the more we lose that pure reverence and fear of the lord, the more our society will fall into ruin.

I'm not against telling stories when preaching, I'm just saying we don't need to exaggerate, and sometimes we have gotten so used it that we don't even realize we are doing it. We have all done this one time or another, I have even done it myself. We don't need stories to get people fired up or cry. When the fire of God is burning people don't need to be entertained, and the stage lighting and the kind of music we use becomes irrelevant. When the fire of God shoots through your bones you will become like the apostles and have no need for anyone to set the atmosphere for you. We often hear the phrase "setting the atmosphere," but wait a minute, the reason why we have to set the atmosphere is because we are not constantly on fire. When you are burning the atmosphere is already set. When our Lord Jesus Christ walked the earth, he didn't need anyone to set the atmosphere for him. The bible says he already has an open heaven. And the bible says "The Zeal of the house of the lord has consumed him" (Psalm 69:9).

Church, we have an open heaven. In the book of Matthew 4 when the heavens opened for Jesus Christ at his baptism, the bible didn't say that it closed back up. We still have that open heaven, and God is still speaking through that open heaven. Let's allow him to speak to his people instead of us entertaining people in an attempt to get them excited about God. Fake excitement doesn't translate into a movement of God, but when God stirs up the heart of his people by his spirit it will create an eternal cry in the hearts of men.

5

FIRE OF LOVE-HEARTS ABLAZE

Set me like a seal over your heart, like a seal on your arm. For love is as strong as death, passion as intense as Sheol. The flames of love are flames of fire, a blaze that comes from the LORD. *(Song of Solomon 8:6 ISV)*

Set me as a seal upon thine heart, as a seal upon thine arm: for love *is* strong as death; jealousy *is* cruel as the grave: the coals thereof *are* coals of fire, *which hath* a most vehement flame. *(Song of Solomon 8:6 KJV)*

Have you ever heard the phrase "Keep the love flame burning"? Well, there is a truth to that in both the physical realm and in the spiritual realm regarding our relationship with others and with our Father.

There is a love that is supernatural that the Father manifested through the power of his Holy Spirit in the 2nd chapter of Acts when tongues of FIRE fell upon the heads of the people waiting in the upper room for the promise of the Holy Spirit. This love was so intense it caused 120 people to be radically transformed instantly. They were said to be like drunk people because their senses were so heightened with the Fire of the Holy Spirit. This promised Holy Spirit caused normal fishermen, tax collectors, and blind beggars to instantaneously become crazed preachers of the gospel who had such great power in their hands that the blind saw instantly, the crippled walked and the dumb spoke. What would cause a person to leave everything they own, their families, careers and passion for life and follow this miracle worker named Jesus? It was love. This fire of love comes from the Lord and it is the supernatural love that he first loved us (1 John 4:19) by which after we receive his grace, we in return love him back. Jesus Christ prayed in John 17, "Father that the same love that you have loved me with be in them." This love creates oneness, when you have the love of God in you, you will become a living sacrifice unto the Lord. Jesus asked Peter, do you love me?

You see, without love your relationship with God becomes nothing more than a religious obligation. Love is expressed in action and if someone has to chase you down and manipulate you to give to God, come to church or even spend time with God that shows you are not in love with Him. That's why Jesus

Christ said in Revelation that you have lost your first love. That first love is a burning love, a COMPELLING LOVE, and is a love that moves you into action. A love that makes you want to hazard your life for the sake of the kingdom of God. But sadly enough, we say we love God but we really don't, remember Revelation 11. They loved not their lives unto death, and that's the problem with some Christians; we don't love God even unto death, instead we love our lives more than we love Jesus, and it shows by the priorities you have in your life. For some God is not even in the top five list of priorities in their life. For some their job is their priority and for others it is their husbands or wives, children or even self. In this kingdom of God there is only one KING and that's Jesus Christ, and any other thing or person you are trying to make king in your life becomes idolatry. Jesus stated that whosoever loves anything more than they love God is not worthy of the kingdom. This kind of love comes from God; it comes as a result of total consumption of the presence of God. When you become a place of habitation for God you become someone that loves God with all your heart and soul. And sometimes we become so blinded with self-righteousness that we don't really ask ourselves "do I really love Jesus?" That's the question we all need to ask ourselves, and based on your priorities you will pretty much know what the answer is. Jesus said to Peter "if you love me feed my sheep."

6

CALLED TO FELLOWSHIP

"That I may know him, and the power of his resurrection, and the fellowship of his sufferings, being made conformable unto his death." *(Philippians 3:10)*

When you come to a clear revelation and understanding of what God really desires from you, it will blow your mind that this mighty God would desire such a thing from you.

People often say they are seeking God, spending time with God, and in their prayers they are asking for God's power and presence. This just goes to show their mindset and that what they really want from God is the power, anointing and blessings of God. They want to be used by God to do mighty works, so they stay in his presence just to get it without a clear understanding of the desires of God. His desire is fellowship with him and everything that happens from there is just the residue of his that fellowship.

In Mark 3:13-15, Jesus Christ called his disciples that they might FIRST be with him and then sent them out.

What is your motive for spending time with God? Some of us who are ministers study and pray because we have to preach. But what happens when we don't have to preach?

One time my wife and I were in London to minister in a regional conference, and while we were there, I was praying, studying and crying out to God for the manifestation of his presence, and while I was laying down praying, the spirit of God asked me "What is your motive for spending this time with me? Are you studying and praying because you have to preach tomorrow, or are you doing it because you love spending time with me? If there were no preaching engagements would you still be spending this time with me? If you never preached again would you still be in my presence fellowshipping with me? I created you first for fellowship with me before anything else.

That hit home for me, because I had never thought about that before. Of course, God knows the answer to that question, which, looking back, I saw that I tended to spend more time with Jesus when I have to preach.

The sad truth is many of us are not even spending that time with him at all. Some are living in past glory, they are still operating from the place of old wine.

Jesus says "on that day I will say to them depart from me I never knew you," (Matthew 7:23) and they will say we did all kinds of miracle in your name, cast out devil in your name. A sense of entitlement has taken over this generation and we want everything to be handed to us because we think we deserve it. I call this a microwave generation. When Jesus says "I never knew you" it means you never sought a relationship with him, it takes fellowship to know people. You don't just know people from meeting them for the first time and neither do you know them by spending time with them infrequently like once a month. Knowing comes as a result of fellowship, when was the last time you came into the presence of God and said, "God, I don't need anything from you. I just miss spending time with you, and I just want to fellowship with you without the pressure of having to get a sermon ready or fulfilling my religious obligation of praying and reading my bible every day."

In Exodus, Moses asked God to show him his glory, and what was God's response? God says you will not see my face, so what Moses was asking for was a personal encounter with God. Most of our preachers and leaders haven't had that personal encounter with God, and that's why we can't teach or direct people to that realm with God. Moses desired that personal time with God, asking nothing in return, he just loves that God that had been so good to him. And God says you will not see my face but my back, and I will hide you in a rock by me. We know that Jesus Christ is the ROCK, so God was introducing Moses to Jesus Christ. When you are in love with Jesus Christ, your heart will burn and desire to fellowship with him. Love is the motivation. Jesus prayed in John 17, "Father may this love that is in us dwell in them." Love makes you become one with God, love moved Jesus Christ to pursue you and give his life for a relationship with you. Do you think that the main reason he gave his life was just for the healing of your body or deliverance? That's part of it, but the main reason Jesus Christ gave his life was to restore the relationship man had with God in the Garden of Eden. And what did they have? The answer is fellowship and a relationship. I pray that while you are reading this book that our Father will open your eyes to see and understand what I'm saying. You were made for love and fellowship.

In John 4, Jesus says that now is the hour and time when God is seeking for those who will worship God in truth and spirit. He seeks them and desires that true worshippers will emerge. When I'm talking about worshippers I'm not talking about singing, I'm talking about people who are sold out to God. If our leaders are not sold out to God it becomes a problem because your followers will always pattern themselves after their leader. I pray every day to God that I don't want to pastor a lukewarm church. Instead I want to be a leader that will lead people into pursuing the heart of God. Jesus, talking about John the Baptist asked the people what they went to see, a man with golden apparel? He said those kinds of people are in the palace because they are a generation that wants to settle for the things of this world, a generation more interested in how they look than desiring God. A generation that is more interested in building a megachurch than fellowshipping with the king, a generation that is more interested in driving the most expensive cars and having the biggest houses than they are in having a relationship with God. What are you seeking in your life?

Wrong motives can also hinder us from stepping into the fullness of God. We often think what will bring this generation into the kingdom is programs, events and more church buses, lighting or a nice church complex. No, that's not what will bring this generation into the kingdom of God. This generation wants to see the difference between us and them. How can you expect them to think they need God when you are no different than they are? What will bring this generation into the kingdom of God is the presence of God, when we become the light we are supposed to be; but you can't be the light if you have not been lit up.

Of the ten virgins in Matthew 25, five of them had oil and five didn't. Oil represents the anointing or presence of God which comes as a result of fellowshipping with the giver of this oil. When you want to charge the battery on your phone you have to plug it into a power outlet. God is the one that pours this oil on you to enable the flame to burn, but if you don't spend time with him you won't have any flame no matter how much you try to fake it.

The earth is still waiting for sold out lovers of Jesus Christ to emerge those who are in total fellowship with

Jesus Christ; those that will give up everything just to spend time with God. I often hear people make excuses why they are not in church. When there is snow here in America people stay home from church, but somehow they still go to work. It is amazing how they can leave a warm house to get into a warm car to drive to a warm church building, but they say it is too cold outside.

I've hear people tell me that they don't have time to church because they work too much. That just shows you their heart and priority. Anything that replaces God in our lives is idolatry, including working and money. May the day never come when I would exalt anything above God, be it a job or anything at all. God is first in my life and will always remain first. Every job that I have ever held, I always told them that I couldn't work on Sundays. Not because I was being religious but because I love spending time with God's people in the house of God.

David said "I was glad when they said unto me, let us go unto the house of the Lord." When Jesus Christ went into the temple and threw them all out it was said, the ZEAL of the house of the Lord has consumed me.

7

SPIRITS AT WAR- FIGHTING TO MAINTAIN THE VICTORY

"The LORD is a man of war: the LORD is his name."
(Exodus 15:3)

If you seek to desire to change and influence your natural realm you have to be able to go and take charge of the spiritual realm. If God were to open your eyes into the spiritual realm, you would realize that there is a battle going on every single second of the day. We know that Jesus has won the battle and emerged triumphant over the enemy. As a result, he has all the authority over heaven and earth, so when we engage in spiritual battle, we are maintaining the authority that Jesus Christ has already given to us. We're to maintain the victorious belt that we were given, yet many times churches don't want to speak about spiritual warfare, and the number one reason is because they are afraid. They assume that if they just ignore the subject, the devil will leave them alone. But they are making a grave mistake because he bothers and attacks anybody that he can, especially Christians. His job description is to make your life miserable. *The thief comes only to steal and kill and destroy; but I (Jesus) have come that they may have life, and have it to the full (John 10:10).* So you better get out of your defensive mode and switch over to offensive mode because when you do that, you can destroy all the plans and tactics of the enemy. But when you remain in defensive mode and don't want to hear any evil or speak any evil because you're afraid the demons are going to chase you down, well, they are already waiting to chase you down so you better be prepared.

Step into your authority and take charge in the spirit realm. The reason I teach on spiritual warfare and teach on the demonic and angelic realms is not to scare anybody or become an obsession. My job is to teach believers that the spiritual realm is very real and equip them to deal with the demons who live here on earth until the appointed time comes when they will be destroyed forever. It is vital that God's people grasp that satan and his demons not only want to destroy their lives, they delight in doing so. When the demons wreak havoc in your life they get more rank in the spiritual realm. Jesus talked about spiritual warfare, and the heart of God in spiritual warfare is to expose the enemy's plans and tactics. If Jesus wanted to ignore it, he wouldn't have mentioned its existence. Rather, all throughout the gospels, Jesus was casting out devils and rebuking evil spirits. Why was Jesus doing that? He said to his disciples, I give you power to cast out devils. Why did Jesus give us that command if the devils weren't harming people's lives? Why do we need to cast them out then? Why don't we just hand our power over to them then? Because that's what we're doing when we don't exercise spiritual authority over the demonic realm. There are different misconceptions about demons. We know that they are fallen angels, and I've heard them referred to as dark personalities, dark shadows, ghosts and so on but they are spirit individuals with their own distinct personalities.

We need to understand that what makes someone a person is not our physical body but our senses, will, and decision making abilities and emotions. These beings have personalities. Do you believe that the things that happen in your life are just a coincidence? We cannot shift the responsibility of living for Christ over to satan, blaming him for every sin we commit. We can't blame the enemy for making us sin because it is our will that makes us commit sins. The enemy doesn't have power over your will. God gave you the ability to make a choice. You have a will and the ability to make your own decisions, and God will not overstep your ability or will.

The word devil comes from the Greek word Diablos, meaning liar, enemy or false accuser. The devil is a thought thrower who comes and throws a thought into your mind. James says that God doesn't tempt a man, but the enemy comes in and whispers thoughts and seeds into your mind. And remember, when you are being tempted, do not say, "God is tempting me." God is never tempted to do wrong, and he never tempts anyone else (James 1:13 NLT). That is why we need to have the mind of Christ, and how do we have the mind of Christ; by renewing our mind with the word of God. When we start renewing our mind with the word of God, then the enemy comes and tries to make accusations. The bible calls him the accuser of the brethren in Revelation 12:10.

Have you ever noticed how when you decide to pray, suddenly your mind begins to fill with things that have happened over the past several years all at once? It's because the enemy is trying to accuse you before the Father, but he cannot go into your mind and manipulate it unless he is given an open door to do that. There are portals that open up entry ways to the enemy in our lives and when the portals are opened, he comes in and tries to take ownership. But we know that he cannot do that because he is not our creator or Father. However, he tries to overstep our authority and take over our minds because he needs bodies to operate through. We have to get to the place where we take responsibility for our sins. We cannot be consumed with our own thoughts or wills and allow sin to consume our minds and then appear before God and excuse it by saying the devil made me do it. Who are these demons that we're talking about?

Here are several scripture references in which Jesus speaks about demons and casting them out.

"And his fame went throughout all Syria: and they brought unto him all sick people that were taken with divers diseases and torments, and those which were possessed with devils, and those which were lunatic, and those that had the palsy; and he healed them." *(Matthew 4:24)*

"When the even was come, they brought unto him many that were possessed with devils: and he cast out the spirits with his word, and healed all that were sick: That it might be fulfilled which was spoken by Esaias the prophet, saying, Himself took our infirmities, and bare our sicknesses. Now when Jesus saw great multitudes about him, he gave commandment to depart unto the other side. And a certain scribe came, and said unto him, Master, I will follow thee whithersoever thou goest. And Jesus saith unto him, The foxes have holes, and the birds of the air have nests; but the Son of man hath not where to lay his head. And another of his disciples said unto him, Lord, suffer me first to go and bury my father. But Jesus said unto him, Follow me; and let the dead bury their dead. And when he was entered into a ship, his disciples followed him. And, behold, there arose a great tempest in the sea, insomuch that the ship was covered with the waves: but he was asleep. And his

disciples came to him, and awoke him, saying, Lord, save us: we perish. And he saith unto them, Why are ye fearful, O ye of little faith? Then he arose, and rebuked the winds and the sea; and there was a great calm. But the men marvelled, saying, What manner of man is this, that even the winds and the sea obey him! And when he was come to the other side into the country of the Gergesenes, there met him two possessed with devils, coming out of the tombs, exceeding fierce, so that no man might pass by that way. And, behold, they cried out, saying, What have we to do with thee, Jesus, thou Son of God? art thou come hither to torment us before the time? And there was a good way off from them an herd of many swine feeding. So the devils besought him, saying, If thou cast us out, suffer us to go away into the herd of swine. And he said unto them, Go. And when they were come out, they went into the herd of swine: and, behold, the whole herd of swine ran violently down a steep place into the sea, and perished in the waters. And they that kept them fled, and went their ways into the city, and told everything, and what was befallen to the possessed of the devils." (Matthew 8:16-33)

"As they went out, behold, they brought to him a dumb man possessed with a devil. And when the devil was cast out, the dumb spake: and the multitudes marvelled, saying, It was never so seen in Israel. But the Pharisees said, He casteth out devils through the prince of the devils." (Matthew 9:32-34)

"For John came neither eating nor drinking, and they say, He hath a devil." (Matthew 11:18)

"And at even, when the sun did set, they brought unto him all that were diseased, and them that were possessed with devils." (Mark 1:32)

"And to have power to heal sicknesses, and to cast out devils: And Simon he surnamed Peter; And James the son of Zebedee, and John the brother of James; and he surnamed them Boanerges, which is, The sons of thunder: And Andrew, and Philip, and Bartholomew, and Matthew, and Thomas, and James the son of Alphaeus, and Thaddaeus, and Simon the Canaanite, And Judas Iscariot, which also betrayed him: and they went into an house. And the multitude cometh together again, so that they could not so much as eat bread. And when his friends heard of it, they went out to lay hold on him: for they said, He is beside himself. And the scribes which came down from Jerusalem said, He hath Beelzebub, and by the prince of the devils casteth he out devils." (Mark 3:15-22)

"And they cast out many devils, and anointed with oil many that were sick, and healed them." (Mark 6:13)

"The woman was a Greek, a Syrophenician by nation; and she besought him that he would cast forth the devil out of her daughter." (Mark 7:26)

There are different names given by the bible for these spirits, and these names can help us understand their jobs. We need to understand their jobs so that we can defeat them. In Ephesians 6, Paul speaks about putting on the armor of God so that we can know and defeat the wiles of the enemy. The word wiles in Greek means strategy. There are different strategies the enemy attempts to use in order to gain access into your life. If one doesn't work, he goes and tries a different form of the main weakness you may be struggling with. Paul said in Hebrews 12 we should lay aside every sin and weights that easily besets you. The enemy knows your weakness and he tries to use it against you. A weight is something in your life that may not be a sin, but it hinders your being able to serve God. What is a weight for you may not be a weight for me and vice versa.

For example, there was a young man called to the ministry who would not play basketball while in Bible college. The reason was that he was so good playing basketball in high school that a scout offered him a full scholarship to a prestigious college. He told the teachers he did not want to play on the team, even though it was just for fun because he didn't want to be tempted to quit serving God and go back to the world. You need to examine your life and realize what weights the devil can use to prevent you from serving him. He waits until your defenses are down so that he can strike, but when we understand his tactics and strategies we can overcome them. Every second of every day the enemy is working to set you up with the things he feels he can get you with. Have you ever gotten into a situation and realized it was a set up? You know you've been set up by Satan to fail? Well, Glory be to God because whenever he sets us up, God is able to move things and transform them around for his own glory!

In I Kings 22:21-22 the bible speaks of a lying spirit. While reading this passage, I was contemplating how a King could go to war and make up his mind about what he is supposed to do. A lot of times, we come to God with our minds already made up about what we want, but we ask him what he wants to do. He was trying to manipulate getting a blessing from God. The bible said God asked "what are we going to do to this King?" And then the lying spirit entered into the mouths of the prophets which prophesied lies to him. So the prophets showed up and gave these kings lies and told him that he would win the war, which is what the king wanted to hear. He didn't want to know the truth, he only wanted to win the war. The king said that he knew of a man named Micah who would tell him the truth so he called for him. The servants brought Micah in to give the King a word and Micah told him he would win the war, but the King knew he wasn't giving the true word, and so he asked him a second time and Micah prophesied that he would lose the war.

We can see here that a lying spirit's job is to twist, distort, and dilute the truth into a lie. Have you ever talked to somebody and known 100% what you just said to the person, but the person you were speaking to heard something completely different? This lying spirit stands in between our communications so that when you say something, it becomes garbled and unclear, causing a person to hear something different than what you just said. That is why the bible is very clear on what we are to say and tells us not to allow any evil communication to proceed out of your mouth (Ephesians 4:29). Because it opens up a portal for the lying spirit to come in and twist what you just said.

The lying spirit is everywhere deceiving people today, even in the church where doctrines are being taught that are not found in the Bible, and lying spirits are twisting the Word of God. People are pulling a few scriptures out of the Bible that they like while ignoring the rest. Another thing the lying spirit does is to come in and tell a person lies about themselves that they're ugly, nobody likes you, and your life is a waste. These are lies because they come from the father of lies. How can we believe the lies of the enemy and think that anything he says is true? The enemy tells you the opposite of truth, if he says you're not worth anything then the opposite is true, you are valuable. The lies come in to twist a person's mind and it causes a person to see things differently. Have you ever tried to explain something simple to a person but no matter how hard you try they just cannot seem to understand it? It's because the enemy has twisted their mind through the lying spirit. This spirit is doing a lot of damage in the church by telling believers lies about each other and causing division while trying to destroy the work of God. It hinders you from truth, because truth sets you free (John 8:32). If they get access to your mind, they can control your life. It's very important that you watch what you believe and hear. Faith comes by hearing and hearing the word of God (Romans 10:17). The same way the enemy speaks and fear enters, insecurity and rejection comes as a result of listening to lies. We need to guard our minds so that he cannot gain access to it.

The familiar spirit works in different ways which are familiar to you. It can show up in different ways that you trust, believe in, and are familiar with. They will use them in order to come in and destroy you. Many times, the familiar spirit comes into your life through a person that you trust, and then when it begins to destroy things in your life you find yourself wondering how it happened? The bible speaks of the armor of God in Ephesians 6, and the first piece is the helmet. Why do we need a helmet; to protect our head. When you're on a motorcycle, you must wear a helmet in case of an accident so that your head doesn't get crushed. The helmet protects you from every arrow that the enemy tries to shoot into your mind.

When you have on the helmet of salvation, you are protected from every bad seed the enemy tries to sow into your mind. Jesus talked about sowing seeds in a parable. When we allow these seeds to grow, before we know it those thoughts manifest themselves in the natural realm. When I caught this understanding, and the enemy tries to shoot a thought into my head, I immediately voice out and rebuke him in the name of Jesus. Whenever I do, I can feel something lift off my mind. The first time it happened, I literally felt the arrow leave my mind, so I put on my helmet and recognize when he's trying to shoot and I can defeat him.

In Leviticus 19:31 & Deuteronomy 4:19 it talks of the spirit of fortune. If you've ever gone to a fortune teller, it is the spirit behind that power. They give false words about your destiny by trying to bring spiritual alignment with the moon, sun, and stars and numbers. I have seen believers open up themselves to this spirit which also comes with deception and disguises itself by telling people what they want to hear. In the prophetic movement in the church, I've witnessed people giving false words where everything is perfect and good, and we can't discern enough to know the truth into their lives.

Imagine if true prophets began giving words of warning and heeding people away from the enemy back to God, there would be a lot fewer casualties in the body of Christ today. If somebody that were to prophesy that the enemy was planning so that you were to have a car accident tomorrow, God would reveal it so that you can pray and cancel it to prevent it from happening. I've had many warning dreams where the Lord prevented an accident by revealing the plan of the enemy so that I could pray against it. God never allows anything to happen without first revealing it to his servants (Amos 3:7). We need to understand that we have the true spirit of God inside of us and the enemy is a counterfeit. He is only trying to create and make something happen that isn't there. So if you've ever gone to a fortune teller before, you need to repent and cancel out their predictions under the blood in Jesus' name.

The bible talks about evil spirits in Luke 7:21 and Acts 19:12-16. In Acts 19, the seven sons of Sceva went to a man who was possessed with an evil spirit and tried to cast the spirit out, but they didn't have the clear understanding of who they were. In spiritual warfare you must understand who you are in Christ. If you are in the United States Marine Corps or US Army and you walk into the enemy's camp in Afghanistan and they ask you who you are and you say you don't know, they're going to turn against you quick.

The first thing in spiritual warfare is knowing your position in Christ, because then you can defeat any strategy the enemy brings against you. The sons of Sceva tried to cast out these devils by saying "In the name of Jesus that Paul preached about." They didn't know Jesus personally but they heard Paul preaching about him. The evil spirit said, "Jesus I know, Paul I know but who are you." You can't go into the enemy's camp without an identity. You need an identity that is higher up than the enemy's camp in order to gain the victory. So the evil spirit tore them apart and they ran off naked, and fear came upon people because they witnessed an attempt at deliverance ministry with people who didn't know who the enemy was, when in actuality Deliverance ministry is simple, because you get to work with a power that doesn't belong to you.

What we have is a delegated authority. We are delegates of heaven and when we go into the enemy's camp, we are a delegate of heaven. The authority has been given over and handed to us by Jesus Christ.

The unclean spirit has done a lot in the church; it is unholy, immoral and filthy. We see a lot of pastors addicted to porn, believing they are clean but are still living in filth every single day. There are several people who are carrying this seducing spirit. If you are sensitive to the spiritual realm, you can sense it very clearly on the person. The enemy is trying to seduce the church into an unholy lifestyle because the bible says if the hedge is broken, the serpent will bite (Ecclesiastes 10:8).

The only way that the enemy can get past the hedge of protection is by sin through unholy and unclean things in our lives. When those things enter in, the holiness and power of God built around us begins to break and the enemy comes in and strikes. The bible says give no room to the devil (Ephesians 4:27). Anything that opens up the door to the enemy cannot be allowed or he will take over completely. He doesn't come into a person's life to negotiate but to take over, give him no room! How does the seducing spirit come in? As something beautiful and tempting, looking very good and nice. The enemy lays out an offer, just like when Jesus was fasting and the enemy came and offered Jesus the whole world in exchange for worshipping him. He tried to seduce Jesus with the things and pleasures of this earth. That is the seducing spirit which pulls our eyes off of God and onto the things of this world. Our eyes should be looking unto Jesus, the author and finisher of our faith (Hebrews 12:2). So its job is to twist your eyes from looking up, to looking down. Do not allow the unclean spirit to come into your life because it opens the door to destruction and death through sickness and cancer, and it's a struggle to get out. Before you know it, you're struggling, trying so hard to pull yourself out of the trap and wondering how you ever got there in the first place.

An unclean spirit works with the seducing spirit because once you're seduced to the things of the world, the unclean spirit takes over and the person lives in filth before God. We need to know that the eyes of God are so holy that he cannot behold iniquity (Habakkuk 1:13). Righteousness and holiness are what the Father requires from his children. I Timothy 1 says that in the last days people will become seduced and we see that today. People want fame, fortune, wealth and things that are beautiful to the eye. You will see a picture of what you want. Why did satan use this tactic against Jesus when he offered him the beauty of the world in exchange for worship? He knew Jesus was the son of God. When he said to Jesus "If you are the son of God turn these stones into bread" He knew Jesus was the messiah and son of God, but he wanted Jesus to be tempted by questioning who he was. Jesus is Lord so he is the truth, and he already knew this tactic. Everything satan was trying to offer him was his anyway, but satan was trying to do away with the cross. Angels of darkness masquerading as angels of light try to make things look like it's the will of God when in actuality they are trying to take you out of God's will. We must ask God to open our eyes to see the strategies of the enemy and to know the difference between him and God. Ask God for clarity to hear his voice and be able to know and discern what is from God and what is not. When you have discernment, you can know the tactics of the enemy. It may look and sound good, and be a great offer, but it is not God's will for your life. A seducing spirit will always push you away from God and into the carnality of the world. It wants you to be carnal and lose all spiritual discernment and sensitivity. We have a God that is powerful enough to defeat everything the enemy tries to bring our way.

The spirit of destruction, Abaddon and Apollyon in Hebrew and Greek, comes into a home and its job is to break down the family. When problems are occurring in families there is a spiritual being behind it. We can battle that spirit specifically. You have to understand the spirit that is involved so we can target it directly. This spirit's job is to destroy marriages, families, cities, and nations. We see suicides and murders in our cities and we don't want to go to spiritual war over it. If we just engaged in spiritual warfare, God will reveal to us whenever a person is going to commit suicide and we can battle it in prayer and tear it down. Because people don't believe in spiritual warfare, everyone has gone his own way and when we turn on the news and hear of deaths every day we just turn our ears away.

We just received news today, during our annual spiritual warfare conference that two teenagers in our city committed suicide. How long will we allow this to happen? There are several spirits that lead to this such as depression, rejection, drug use, and alcohol and then the spirit of destruction comes in to take the person out. If the church was spiritual enough, we would not be ignorant of the devices of the enemy and could fight it before it happens.

Five or six years ago, I was sleeping at night when I received a tap on my leg, and I knew it was a cue to pray. When I woke up, I heard audibly, "you need to pray against the spirit of death." I didn't know who to pray for specifically but I began to wage war in prayer against the spirit of death throughout the night. I took authority and broke the back of the power in the spirit realm, and I was so excited that God could trust me enough that he would wake me up and tell me to pray for something like that. I went about my life and forgot about it and then two weeks later I got a call from my Dad, who told me that my younger brother had almost died. What had happed was that In Africa, the fences built around houses are very tall in order to protect against armed robbers. They put sharp objects such as broken bottles and knives at the top of the fence to keep robbers away. My kid brother had climbed a wall to get a mango off of the tree when his hand got stuck and he fell directly onto the broken bottles on the fence. When my Father said that, immediately the scripture that came into my spirit was when Jesus told

Peter in Luke 22:31 that Satan had wanted to sift him like wheat, but He had prayed for him. My Dad said that my brother passed out from bleeding so heavily and couldn't get down. There is no ambulance or 911 service in Africa. My Dad is in his 70s and unable to physically climb up that 30 foot wall so he began to panic and ran out into the streets to scream for someone to help him. The strangest thing was that these men came to help but everybody else just stood there and wouldn't move. My Dad knew that the enemy was trying to kill my brother so he started praying immediately when suddenly the men jumped the wall as warriors and pulled him down onto their shoulders and ran him to the hospital by foot because they had no car. When they got to the hospital, thank God for the prayers, his life was saved. After my Dad told me that story, I cried because I knew that night, the life of my brother was in my hands. If I would have made a mistake that night and went to sleep, what would have happened to this kid? Church, we can take care of these problems in the spiritual realm. Counseling has not been able to help these people. Programs cannot help people. We the church, are the only ones who have the hope they need, which is Jesus Christ, and when we wage spiritual warfare, the natural realm will respond. We can pull down whatever stronghold is trying to take down our lives and the lives of our families and loved ones through the power and blood of Jesus Christ. It is noteworthy that our youth are in extreme danger from the spirit of destruction which is moving through our cities looking for the slightest opening to come in and destroy them through drugs, alcohol and other things, but we can change all that. If God is able to hear our prayers and save the lives of those we pray for, we owe them that. We just have to come out of our comfort zones and stop thinking about ourselves. Jesus said you cannot come into a strongman's house and take his belongings without first binding the strongman. That is why the solutions of the world such as counseling and twelve step programs do not have permanent effects because they do not have the power and authority to bind the strongman.

Thank God for programs and counselors, they are needed, but we as the church must also do our own part. The world can handle the physical things, and we can handle the spiritual things. What if we get on our knees and start commanding all of the spiritual demonic powers to leave our cities? We can send them all out into exile. We can do that. Just look at what happened when Jesus walked up to the man with legions of demons in Gadera. This man was possessed with up to 6,000 demons, who were trying to destroy him through cutting himself with stones. Just like, today, there are millions of young people cutting themselves every day bleeding, and we make excuses for them by saying they are just having emotional problems. They are affected by the same demon that was afflicting this man in the bible who was cutting himself and overtaken by the enemy, screaming and crying, but he couldn't stop. When Jesus showed up and began to walk towards him, the man ran towards Jesus then bowed down and said to Jesus "I know that you are the son of God, have you come to destroy us?" The demons knew their time had come to leave the man, they said to Jesus "Please don't send us out of the country." They didn't want to leave the city. Why would Jesus grant their request? The city would have been a lot better off without all those demons there. Jesus allowed them to enter into the swine instead of leaving the region. They ran violently into the ocean, and the spirit violently destroyed the pigs and drowned them in the ocean. We need to send them out of our regions, counties, cities and nations so that the lives of our young people will be saved. Imagine how the parents of these children must feel when they walk into their teenager's bedroom and see their son hanging from the ceiling and have to watch their sons and daughters die because some demons that have gotten control of them. When the spirit of destruction comes in, it could happen to anybody. The amazing thing is that we have what it takes, the ability, the anointing, and the strength and power to do that because Jesus Christ has given us the power to cast out demons. We're waiting for God to come down and exercise all the demons out of people but he's waiting for us to do it. He already did it when he took the power from satan and gave it to us.

We're going to have questions to answer and explanations to give when we stand before God. When God gave us the cities, the bible says that whatever the soles of our feet touches, we shall possess (Joshua 1:3). Instead, many of us will stand before God and say "well God, I went to church every Sunday." We are not called to be mere church attendees but to make an impact in this generation. We are not created to be bystanders but partakers in this end time army. If God didn't need you here on earth, you wouldn't be here, but he needs you and wants to use you to subdue the powers of the enemy.

When the spirit of destruction gets ahold of a city, it travels from region to region and can cause a lot of problems and catastrophes in families. Why is there so much divorce in this nation? The enemy is breaking down the family unit and we just sit back and watch. It's time to rise up and take our places of authority in Jesus Christ. After all, Jesus said we are the salt and light of the world. We can bring the taste back to the earth. When we begin to pray and pull down strongholds, we will see more freedom in our lives and families when we pray and speak over the four corners of our cities and families. We speak to the north, south, east, and west and each direction and command every power and principality to bow in Jesus' name. All authority in heaven and earth has been given to Jesus and then to us. They must bow down to that authority since we have Jesus Christ inside of us. Whatever you bind on earth is bound in heaven and when we speak it shall be done. When two or more agree and believe something, it shall happen. We pull down every stronghold, power of darkness, and satanic influence over this city and pull down the strongman in our cities and families. It's time for war!!!

"He teacheth my hands to war, so that a bow of steel is broken by mine arms." *(Psalm 18:34)*

The mentality that a warrior goes to battle with will determine the technique, approach and the extent to how vigorous he will fight. One of the best pieces of advice to apply to spiritual warfare comes from one of the greatest military leaders of all time, General George S. Patton. In his memoirs, *"War as I Knew It,"* he said "when under attack advance, artillery very seldom shortens its range." In other words, when satan and his forces are attacking don't retreat, advance.

What so many believers don't understand, and often times we may say it but don't really realize or believe what we are saying is that Jesus Christ HAS won the battle for us. We are only fighting to maintain the victory that Jesus Christ has given us. Jesus says, "Little children do not be afraid I have overcome the world" (John 16:33).

The world overcome is a Greek word Nikao which means to conquer, to carry off to victory, to subdue. So even before Jesus Christ went to the cross he told his disciples that he already overcame the world. Jesus knew that fear would come into their hearts, fear of losing the battle, fear of not having enough strength to fight, and so he told them not to be afraid because he already won the battle for them. That is great news to know that the battle has been won for me without having to go to war. When a heavyweight boxing champion is challenged by someone who wants his belt, the champion goes into the ring with the mentality of fighting to keep his belt because he already has the victory. The devil wants to WIN, BUT YOU ARE GOING TO MAINTAIN YOUR VICTORY because he has already lost.

You are not engaged in spiritual warfare to WIN; you are fighting to keep the victory so that the enemy will not steal the victory you have in Christ Jesus from you. He starts by speaking lies that you will never be free or that you are going through whatever trial you are facing because God is trying to teach you some lessons. God can teach you a lesson without you going through a painful time. The book James says that he doesn't tempt anyone with evil. The bible says whom the son of man sets free is free indeed. You didn't do anything to deserve the freedom that Jesus Christ gave you, it was part of the price that he paid so that you will be free, that's how amazing our God is. Your mind is the breeding battleground of the devil and that's why the bible speaks about having the mind of Christ, and what is the mind of Christ? It is knowing that you already have the victory, knowing that the greatest warrior and the Kings of Kings and Lord of Lords is Christ, the one that fought your battle for you. At his feet every knee will bow, *"His name has been given above every name that at the mention of his name every knee shall bow and every tongue shall confess that he is the Lord" (Philippians 2:9, 10).*

When Jesus Christ gave them power over unclean spirits, it was a delegated authority. He said, "Cast out the devil, heal the sick, cleans the leper, why? Because all authority and power has been given to me" and when they came back rejoicing, he said to them "I see the devil cast out of heaven, do not rejoice just because the devil obeyed you, that's a done deal he doesn't have any option rather to obey, but there is something better to rejoice about and that is your name being written in the book of life."

The important thing to understand is that the language the devil understands is the language of authority and power. When Jesus Christ walked the earth he operated in so much power and authority that he was never afraid of the world. He was never afraid of anything, he even calmed the storm in the ocean to such an extent that even his disciples asked "what manner of man is this that even the ocean hears his voice and they obey him." When you know who you are in Christ, the situation around you will hear your voice and obey. Remember in Genesis 1, when God gave us the dominion and authority to rule the earth and the minute the devil was cast out of heaven God never gave him power over the earth, it was still ours to keep.

As a deliverance minister, I had to understand that the devil is like a roaring lion seeking whom he may devour (I Peter 5:8). The bible says like a roaring lion, but the bible says you have to be népho which is a Greek word for SOBER which means to be calm and collected in spirit. This takes us back to the instruction of Jesus Christ to his disciples to not be afraid. Fear removes you from the right state of mind and makes you vulnerable to attack by the enemy. Fear removes you from trusting in the victory that Jesus Christ has given you and leads you to trust in yourself that you are the one that has to win the battle. Why are you even able to fight in the first place? How do you think you can defeat the demonic realm on your own? The only reason you are able to go into warfare is because Jesus Christ gave you the authority to go.

The United States Army will not go to war without the authorization of the commander-in-chief, who gives them the authority. When they go into battle they go on behalf of America, not on their own as mercenaries. They know that the commander-in-chief is behind them and will provide them all the necessary logistical support they need for that war. Jesus Christ says in *Matthew 28:19 "Lo I am with you through the end of the age,"* but first he says GO. He authorized the offensive attack on the enemy because the whole host of heaven is completely behind us. The bible says we have a whole cloud of witnesses in reserve.

8

FEAR OF LOSING THE BATTLE

"And he answered, fear not: for they that be with us are more than they that be with them." *(II Kings 6: 16)*

Fear is one of the key factors that affect believers. I have come across some believers who believe that the whole world is against them; someone is tapping their phone, someone is following them and trying to kill them. As a result, they live their whole life in fear of the unknown.

Elisha was a man that heard God, he understood the authority that he has in God, and that he has a God behind him. The king of Syria was coming against Israel, and Elisha the prophet was the one telling the king of Israel the enemy's battle plans. He was not a trained officer, warrior or fighter, Elisha didn't know anything about the logistics and tactics involved in fighting. All he knew was there was a God in heaven that has power over all flesh. So when the Syrian King saw Israel outsmarting them, he wondered who was giving them all the information. He was told there was a man called Elisha who is a prophet of God and tells the Israelites all about his plans. This is how God operates, he knows all things and that's why Paul says in II Corinthians 2:11 "Lest the devil take advantage of us for we are not ignorant of his devices."

God was revealing to Elisha the plans of the Syrian army and because of that Israel became untouchable. You are untouchable when you allow the spirit of God to bring to you the revelation of God, and revelation comes as a result of intimacy with He that knows all things. He says, call upon me in the days of trouble and I will show you the things to come.

So when the King of Syria knew that Elisha was giving out his plans he wanted to kill Elisha and sent horses and chariots along with a great host; and they came by night and compassed the city about and when the servant of Elisha woke up in the morning and saw all the army against them, he was very afraid, his spiritual eyes were closed so that he could only see the physical and not the spiritual realm. Elisha operated in both realms, and that's why our daily prayer should be that God will open our eyes to the spiritual realm; because how can we fight the spiritual realm without knowing what's out there to fight. Paul's says *"that the eyes of your understanding be enlightened so that you will see the hope of your calling" (Ephesians 1:18).*

Ephesians 3:10 then goes on to say, *"To the intent that now unto the principalities and powers in heavenly places might be known by the church the manifold wisdom of God."*

The heart of God is for you to know what's going on in the spiritual realm because if you do, it will bring you to a place of peace in God.

So Elisha prayed and said *"That his eyes will be opened so that he will see that them that are with us are more than those that are against us."* Brethren, we have a great and mighty God and His whole being and very existence is to back you up and protect you. The consumption of your heart to fear is what has been holding you back from being free, and when Elisha's servant saw that the whole host of heaven was behind them, I wonder what was going on in his mind. He probably got fired up and excited, knowing at that point that he could take on the whole world since God is with them.

You are a child of God and he will never leave you nor forsake you. Psalm 91 says that he gives his angels charge over you. The angels of God have been instructed to protect you, to keep their eyes on you and make sure you do not dash your foot against a stone. A thousand shall fall on your left side and ten thousand on your right hand and they shall not come nigh thee.

Psalm 23 says that though you walk through the valley of the shadow of death you will fear no evil because God is with you and His rod and staff comforts you. The rod is a symbol of authority. Most of the time believers don't even realize that God is with them. I have had many people tell me that because they don't feel God, that he is not with them anymore. But understand that in this kingdom things are not based on feelings. The just shall live by faith the bible says, and the word faith means trust, just trusting God that since he says that he will be with you and he will always be there. He won't just one day decide that he doesn't like you anymore and is bored being around you, and so he's going to be taking a break from being around you. Do you even understand that the word of God says that you are hidden in Christ and Christ is hidden in God? A preacher said one day that if the devil wants to destroy you that he would have to operate on God and bring Jesus Christ out, and then operate on Jesus Christ and bring you out and only then can he kill you. I know that's just another way to explain it, but it is not possible for the enemy to do that. He doesn't have the power or authority to do it.

You have a GOD who created the universe, he is the Lord over all things, and there is no other God beside him. Fear is the absence of security in God. The word of God says that perfect love casts out fear. If you say you are a child of God and do not realize that God loves you with perfect love then you will live the rest of your life in uncertainty. The perfect love of God removes fear, but you have to accept that perfect love; the love that sees you where you are at.

From the foundation of the earth, and from the time of man's creation we see in Genesis 1 that man was made in the likeness and image of God. In Genesis,

God says "Let us make man in our image that they would have DOMINION over the earth." The enemy is not in charge. Sometimes we think he is, but from the foundation of the earth, the people that God made to be in charge of the earth were you and me. We were made to have power and dominion over the earth and have the power to change the things around us. When the enemy came in, he stole our identity when he came to Eve and questioned her in the garden. He lied and twisted God's word and caused her to question her identity in God. Eve didn't understand that she was already like God because she was made in his image.

The enemy tells you the opposite of what God says about you. The enemy wanted to separate the man and woman and take away their dominion. We know that the enemy previously dwelt in heaven with the Father and the hosts of angels but what happened was that he said "I will exalt myself above God" but God will not share his glory with anybody. That's why we need to remember that humility is very important in the kingdom because when we allow pride to come in, we are trying to take glory away from God and place it upon ourselves, but he will never share his glory with any man. Because of that pride, there was a war in Heaven and John saw this war taking place in heaven and Michael and the angels began to war against Lucifer and one-third of the angels were deceived and fell from heaven with him (Rev. 12: 4, 7). If he was able to deceive the angels in heaven, how can we think that he won't try the same thing with us? satan fell from heaven to earth and tried to occupy it, but in the beginning God gave the earth to man. We are to steward the earth and have dominion and power over it. The enemy no longer has a place in heaven or earth, that's why he is hanging around in the second heaven because the third heaven and the earth have rejected him. He is a wanderer; he goes around the earth and causes havoc and goes around like a roaring lion seeking whom he can devour (I Peter 5:8). We are the ones that have handed over the earth to the enemy, and that is why he has been doing whatever he wants, but we need to understand that his will is not supposed to be accomplished on the earth, but the will of God as Jesus prayed, thy kingdom come thy will be done on earth as it is in heaven. All we need to do is align our wills with the will of God and this will subdue the enemy. That's why the bible says resist the devil and he will flee from you (James 4:7).

The bible says *you shall know the truth and the truth shall make you free* (John 8:32). The word make "there" means creative ability. The truth has the power to bring revelation to you that will, in turn, change you and everything around you. The enemy hinders the church and people on earth, trying to keep them from the truth because he knows that as soon as the truth comes into your ears, that is the end of him and he will no longer be able to deceive you. So the enemy thought that he destroyed the plan of God, but what he didn't know was that God always has another plan. I'm excited to know that God doesn't just have one plan. When the enemy comes in and tries to destroy God's plans, God implements a new plan. When Christ showed up on earth, the enemy knew that God had another plan to redeem man, but he never thought Jesus Christ would give his life for man. From the time that Jesus was born, satan was bent on destroying him. Even at the age of two, Herod sent out men in the hope that they would kill Jesus. Whenever deliverance comes our way, the enemy always tries to destroy it. Whenever God wants to do something in your life, the enemy will set a person in your way to try and stop it. God is powerful enough to stop satan' plans and that is why Jesus Christ took the keys to hell.

A key represents authority and gives a person access to a place. It's a license of ownership or possession to a place. That is why Jesus said "I have the keys to death, hell and the grave." Even in families, cities, and other places, God will raise up a person and grant them spiritual access to gain entrance where other people cannot go, because they have a spiritual key. When Jesus rose from the dead he said, "all power in heaven and earth was given to me" (Matthew 28:18).

Jesus went and took the dominion and power back from satan and then restored it back to you and me. Jesus didn't need the power, he already had it. Why did he have to go and take it from the enemy? It was because the enemy stole it from you and me. He came to steal, kill and destroy, but Jesus gives this authority and power back to us. The problem is that we refuse to take what Jesus is giving us. He did it all for us, he fought the battle but we don't think we're good enough to have that authority. It was ours to begin with and now he gives it back to us; the power and authority to cast out devils. If we didn't need to cast out devils here on earth, why did Jesus give us the power to do so? In the ministry of Jesus, he was busy preaching, casting out devils and healing the sick. And the three things the enemy does is steal, kill and destroy. Why was Jesus casting out and rebuking devils, commanding them to leave people? All throughout the gospels, he was casting them out and they were leaving, and Jesus gave us that same power. It's no different, Jesus even went on to say "greater things shall you do" (John 14:12). What is the problem then? When the fire and power of God comes we become different people, loaded with the power of God and able to do the things we are supposed to do.

Why are believers afraid of the devil and demons? The reason for this teaching is not to get us obsessed with demons, but to understand that we have power and authority over them. Why do people shake or fear or cry when they sense a devil around them. I've seen so many people cry over the devil, and he doesn't hear that language. The only language the devil understands is authority.

When the Roman centurion came to Jesus and said my servant is sick, the centurion understood authority and recognized the authority conveyed by Jesus, so he knew that he had the power to heal his servant through just a word. Jesus looked at the man and marveled at the response of the man. He said that he had never seen such faith in the land who understood authority. He healed him with a word.

You are a superior officer to the enemy and what drives him mad are people who know who they are and understand that they have authority over him. The only thing he has are lies. The Father seeks relationships with people and the enemy is seeking destruction. There is only one true lion and that is Jesus Christ. (Rev. 5:5). The bible says that satan tries to roar like a lion, but he is a fake. He is trying to scare you. But when he tries to roar, stand in his face and tell him who you are in Christ and he will back off.

Let me let you in on a little secret about lions. When male lions get older up in years, their teeth are often rotted out. Because of this they cannot hunt and kill like they once did. They will get on one side of prey and roar in order to scare them. Hearing the noise they run in the opposite direction into a group of stronger lions who are just waiting for the prey to come right to them.

A lot of times what he tries to do is hinder us from knowing the truth. That is why from childhood people may have told you several lies about yourself such as calling you stupid and worthless. The enemy is trying to steal your identity. He wants to hinder your identity so that when you grow up, you don't know who you are spiritually. Even believers sometimes battle with the question, "Am I really born again?" the spirit bears witness that you are a child of God (Romans 8:16).

If we start listening and feeding into the enemy's lies, before you know it, you are backslidden, out of church, and nowhere to be found. When you understand that you have power and authority over the enemy, your life will be easier because you will see and recognize when the enemy is trying to lie and deceive, and you will learn how to successfully make war against him.

One time I was in my friend's house in Nigeria after a long journey, I fell asleep in the living room while my friend slept in his bedroom. All of a sudden, this demon in the form of a man showed up, sitting at the edge of the bed I was sleeping on. I saw in my mind a black image of a man with long dreadlocks. I was in a light sleep and saw him clearly. I wondered who was sitting by my bed and who it was that was trying to ruin my sleep. I opened my eyes to see if he was gone but he was still there, so I kicked him and said "get off of my bed now," and he got up and walked out of the room. I wasn't afraid at all and went back to sleep because I wasn't going to let any demon ruin my sleep because the bible says, God gives his beloved sleep (Psalm 127:2).

In the morning, I told my friend "something is definitely going on in your house. Did you know there was a demonic being in here?" And I felt by the spirit of God, that this entity had something to do with somebody cursing him from his village (a witch doctor) and he told me "Yes," some people had seen that same being several times in his house and he was scared to be in his own house because of it. I told him "Ok, we're going to take care of that," so I prayed over the home and commanded them all to leave and they did. Why would I be afraid of the enemy when I know that God has given me the power and authority to exorcise him? I'm not afraid to go anywhere. I've gone and performed deliverance on cities and regions, and commanded demons to leave regions. When I was first being trained under a pastor in deliverance ministry in Africa, he took me to do a village deliverance on the main principality in the area. They had erected a shrine for it, and as we stood there I was keeping my eyes open while praying. I stood behind the pastor because I was scared to even go near the shrine. The idol was supposed to be the most powerful idol in the city and I went in with the pastor. Within 10-15 minutes it was done, and we set it on fire and left the area. It was so cool to be a part of something like that for my first time. The same idol that everyone was afraid of, we burned to the ground. People in the village were required to remove their shoes before going anywhere near the idol or they would drop dead, but we didn't. The same God that my Pastor friend has is the same God that you and I have, and we have the same authority and power. What happens is that the enemy tries to puts fear into our hearts to intimidate us, but we haven't been given the spirit of fear, but of POWER!! (II Timothy 1:7)

You see, God created everything to bring forth after its kind. A lion brings forth a lion, and God brought forth you and me, who are made in his image. We were created in his pattern and image. If you claim that God is your father why are you afraid of the devil? Why haven't we started taking down all the witches in our cities? Why haven't' we started taking tents to the witch's meetings and show forth the power of God over them. We are disappointing God if we don't exercise our dominion. It's his will and desire that we be in charge. WE are seated at the right hand of God with Christ in the heavenly places (Ephesians 2:6). We are here on earth but seated at the right hand of the Father, The right hand signifies a place of authority. That is why Jesus is seated there and in Philippians 2, at the mere mention of the name of Jesus every knee shall bow. The mention of the name Jesus produces power and we are seated with him. We are FAR ABOVE principalities and powers. How is it the witches can come up and try to curse you, and you start shaking and call the pastor?

One time, some local witches left a letter under the door of our church. They were threatening and cursing us, and when I picked up the letter, I spoke over it and shot an arrow in the spirit back to them and went about my business. We are not afraid of them, but the sad thing is that these witches have more boldness than most believers. How can they walk up to the door of the church when we want to turn our heads and act like they don't exist? We are the ones with the real power. We have the real deal and they are deceived, they don't know what they're doing. Just because they can levitate a table we become afraid, when our first response should be "In the name of Jesus, table, I command you to come back down."

Elijah understood exactly what was going on and he told the prophets of Baal that his God was the most powerful and then he went ahead and proved it. He told them to go and get their prophets, which were about 400 false prophets, to stand against a single prophet of God. They weren't even ashamed to take on this challenge. When they showed up, the altars were set up and the false prophets first attempted to summon their God. They started screaming and began cutting themselves for hours until nightfall. They thought that by spilling their blood satan would show up, but they were disappointed because the enemy couldn't show up because the real God was on the scene. At the end of the evening Elijah mocked them and told them maybe their God was asleep. He then challenged them and said "Let the God that answers by fire be God." Then, to prove that what was about to happen was a miracle from God and not some magician's trick, he ordered his altar drenched in water. There was no earthly way that it could possibly burn.

He then called on God and he showed up and consumed his enemies and proved himself. Sometimes we become afraid to call on God because we're not sure whether he will show up or not. So when a witch tries to curse and kill us, we cry because we're not even sure that our God will show up on our behalf. This is a trick of the enemy. satan has been stripped of all power and authority, so they have nothing left but deception. Their lies are to scare you and make you believe they can destroy you, but your life is hidden with Christ and Christ is hidden in God (Colossians 3:3). For the enemy to succeed at destroying you, he first must access God, Christ and then get to you. That is impossible for you are protected under the blood of Jesus. We need to start walking on their earth as superior officers and people who have authority. That is why the enemy messes with us, because we don't walk in our authority.

In the 80s there was a strip of land as big as a city in our village in Africa which was a burial ground where they buried our forefathers and ancestors. The people in the village wanted to cultivate the land for use again and transform it from a burial ground in order to expand the village. Whenever the villagers began to enter that land to work on it, they were literally chased off the land by evil spirits. When I'm talking about these things, if you think I'm joking go on a missions trip with us to Africa and you will see with your own eyes and probably run back to America, never to return. What happened was that nobody could enter this land but my Father. My Dad went to the King of the village and negotiated with him and asked, "If I go in and spiritually cleanse this land, what will you do for me?" The King promised my Dad half of the land if he was able to take care of it, and the village would take the other half. My Dad was very happy and agreed to the deal. He went into prayer and sought the face of God, and God said "Go ahead and take care of it." So in the evening my Dad took his team from the church onto the land and he was literally seeing all of the demons with his eyes. My Dad is a seer and his spiritual eyes are opened to what is going on around him at all times. He began kicking them out of the way and his team witnessed him kicking his legs but didn't see what he was kicking.

They thought he was going crazy, but he was commanding them to leave the land. He called the King the next morning and gave him half of the land, which my family still owns to this day. So the village got their half and we haven't used ours because it's so big. Not wanting the land to go to waste, he allowed people from the village to grow food on it.

When we understand who we are, we then understand that we have what it takes to take the enemy down. Jesus wasn't afraid of them because he knew all he needed to do was to speak a word and they would immediately obey. Isn't it amazing to know that we have that same authority? What other confirmation do we need? I've heard people say that they will pray about going into deliverance ministry. What kind of prayer is that? God said in his word that we shall cast out demons. He has given us all authority in heaven and on earth. That means that we have the power to declare on earth, and heaven moves on our behalf. We have the power to declare and earth will shake at our request. Whatever we bind on earth is bound in heaven. The angels are waiting for the warriors to arise. They are waiting for us to pray and move.

A lot of our angels have been unemployed for so long because we haven't been able to put them to work. They need something to do. Why would God give us angels if we didn't need them? The angels of the children come before his presence. I have two angels who are waiting to go into battle and they are very fierce. Their swords are drawn and they are just waiting for their orders to deploy for war. They watch the enemy come near us and wait for the command, yet here we are sitting and waiting on them, but we refuse to open our mouths and pray. The whole earth waits for the manifestation of the sons of God (Romans 8:19).

When Daniel prayed, God dispatched an angel to go and answer his prayer. When we pray, God dispatches angels to go and war and they begin to tear strongholds down. There was a release of an angel who was held in the second heaven for Daniel who was held up by the prince of Persia for 21 days. During this time Daniel kept praying and warring in the spirit and finally, Michael showed up for war and the demons fled. Gabriel then went to Daniel and gave him the message and told him that from the first day that he started praying, God heard the prayer but while he was coming, the prince of the air stood in his way. The bible records this event to show us what happens in the spiritual realm when we pray. We might not see it but it's going on. After giving the message to Daniel, the angel went back and helped fight with Michael.

Just like when the soldiers came to capture Jesus, Peter pulled out his sword to kill them but Jesus told Peter that this was not the time for war, but submission. There is a time for war and a time for obedience. There is a difference between fighting and submission. A good warrior knows when to employ each one. All we need to do is submit our will to God and know that he is working all things out for our good. Jesus told Peter, look there are legions of angels around me right now just waiting for a single command from me to fight but it was time for Jesus to submit his will and go to the cross.

A good soldier knows when to shoot and when to hold their fire. If they shoot at the wrong time they can cause the battle to be lost. If we believers can get ahold of this truth, our spiritual warfare strategies will be more effective. There are times that we think the enemy is trying to destroy or kill us, when in actuality we are being disobedient to God and are fighting the air when we should be submitting. Casting down every imagination when our obedience is fulfilled (II Corinthians 10:5).

Have you ever noticed that after man disobeyed God in the garden all the animals began to disobey man. The bible says that all the animals, including the predators like lions used to walk with Adam and he named them all. But when man disobeyed, the animals also rebelled because the natural order had been broken. Obedience is the strongest weapon in our spiritual warfare arsenal. When we obey God, he causes things to work in our life because it's his order. Obedience is better than sacrifice. We have what it takes to live victoriously and we have been given power over unclean sprits.

One of the main spirits I see operating here is the spirit of heaviness which causes depression. People take prescription medications that knock them out of reality and it works until they come down and need to take more, and the cycle continues, causing mood swings. The spirit of heaviness comes as a result of abuse or things that happened in childhood. This opens the door and the person is always down, always angry, and always tired. When we command that spirit of heaviness off of a person they will be free and instead have the garment of praise. We can no longer be controlled by what happened to us 20 or 30 years ago, but we must be controlled by the spirit of the Lord and break those spirits off our lives. God wants to set us free from those things that have hindered us. If you still have problems in life as a result of verbal, physical or sexual abuse and have gone into hiding, we are going to break them off. We can't allow what somebody did to us to destroy our destiny.

Here is a prayer to break off strongholds.

Father, we believe that you have given us the power to be free from everything that has held us down. Jesus, we believe that you have given us the power to break off satanic strongholds that have been used against us in our lives and families. Jesus, I pray that every satanic assignment used against me by the enemy be removed from by the bloodline I have in Jesus' name. I pray the blood of Jesus would come in and cleanse every generational curse and stronghold and reverse every curse in Jesus' name, for you took every curse on our behalf. Father, I thank you, and I ask you right now to release your power and your spirit to bring freedom upon my life and the lives of your people, in Jesus' name, Amen.

9

GOD IS GOD-SATAN IS NOT

"I am the LORD: that is my name: and my glory will I not give to another, neither my praise to graven images." *(Isaiah 42:8)*

"And no marvel; for Satan himself is transformed into an angel of light." *(II Corinthians 11:14)*

God has feelings and he has a personality; he requires and desires a relationship between himself and us. That relationship was broken by Adam, and Jesus Christ restored it when he stood in proxy for our relationship with God. It is perfect that Jesus brought us to the original plan from the foundation of the earth through his blood. We now have in our possession the means to access those things that were stolen and go back to the original relationship man had with God. God had a wonderful plan and purpose when creating man, and he desires to share all that he is with us because his very being is Love and he wants to share his heart's desire and plans with us. Who is man that God would desire a relationship with us?

In Genesis 1:26 the Lord said, "let us make man in our own image." In one definition- man is the image of God. The bible says in Genesis that God created everything by speaking the words and it came to pass. He created the sea, light, and the ground by his words through his infinite supernatural power. Isn't it amazing to see the creation of God and think that he made it all just by the spoken word? When it was time to create man, God said "Let us create man." He created man with the involvement of everything that existed inside of himself. God was speaking to the son, Jesus, as well as the Holy Spirit and himself as the Godhead and they decided to create man in their own image. God didn't create man in the image of an ape, but in the image of himself. When speaking of the image, you can think of an old 35mm camera. When you took the film out of the camera and developed it you could see an image of the original object. Man is supposed to see and realize who we look like. When we look at each other or ourselves in the mirror, we see the likeness of the Father, and we should look like Him. The image of God inside of us is our DNA. We carry the spiritual DNA of God and his likeness, which makes us look like him both physically and spiritually. When you look at a child who looks exactly like his parents it is because of genetics and his DNA. We are a replica of God and everything he created reproduces after its own kind. A lion reproduces a lion, and a monkey reproduces a monkey. We are the reproduction and offspring of God; we do not just merely exist, nor are we something made by random chance from a big bang, but we were created in his image.

Isn't it amazing that the Almighty God, the all-powerful, all-knowing God gave us his own DNA? Isn't it amazing that he wants us to look like him? He's such a proud father. God is so proud of his children that he wanted to make them just like himself. We were created to like what he likes and hate what he hates. That is why your spirit is crying out for your Father at all times, even though your flesh may not want to. Your spirit is connected to him and is calling out to him all the time because your spirit is the image of the Father.

We are always connected with the heart and frequency of heaven. We were created to do and say what the Father says, just like Jesus did at the age of twelve when he left his parents' house to go to the temple and preach. When his parents found him there they asked him, "What were you doing there?" He answered "Don't you know that I go about my father's business?" Everything about Jesus Christ's life was consumed with his Father's life and intentions. We cannot carry God's DNA and be consumed with the things of the earth while not caring about the things of his heart. What does that mean? We are supposed to live like Christ. We are supposed to think, speak and behave like him because that's who we are, but what happened was that we have allowed the enemy to come in and plant wrong seeds inside of us; deceitful seeds that cause us to no longer want to live the way that he created us. David asked the same question, "Who is man that you are so mindful of him?" We need to understand that the reason Jesus Christ came and died on the cross wasn't for our houses, cars, or for skyscrapers, but he came and died for you. Individually, Jesus gave his life for each one of us. We need to see it as a personal thing.

Sometimes we get caught up in teaching that Jesus came and died for the world, which he did, but we need to also meditate on the revelation that it was personally for us. If you were the only lost person in the entire world, Christ would have died to save you. We have to make a personal choice to have a relationship with Jesus and become born again. Jesus became the mediator that brought us into the right relationship with the Father. God doesn't hate you because you fell into sin, he still loves you and his love is unchanging. There is a difference between God loving us and God not being happy with us. God loves us and that does not change, but there are some choices that we make that he doesn't approve of, but that doesn't mean he hates us. It doesn't mean he pushes you away. We are the ones who made the wrong choices, and he doesn't force us to choose life. We have to make that decision ourselves. It's so exciting to know we are not just existing, having no purpose for our life. If God orchestrated all these things on earth, how do you think it could be that you would be here for no reason? Everything he makes is perfect and has a reason for its being here. He made the whole earth before he created man, and when he made man he put us in charge of the earth. The earth was given to man to run and take care of. There is an enemy who is fighting our God given dominion and authority.

"How you are fallen from heaven, O shining star, son of the morning! You have been thrown down to the earth, you who destroyed the nations of the world. For you said to yourself, 'I will ascend to heaven and set my throne above God's stars. I will preside on the mountain of the gods far away in the north. I will climb to the highest heavens and I will be like the Most High.'" (Isaiah 14:12-14)

There are several reasons why the enemy was cast out of heaven and one of them was jealousy. The enemy is jealous of man. lucifer saw that God had created man to be like him, so he wanted to be like God also, but he wanted to be higher than God He was a warrior and worshipper and he was very powerful, but when he began to see God's creation and the angels glorifying God, lucifer began to be jealous. When God made lucifer he was not made in the image of God and neither are the angels. We are the only creation made in God's image. The angels were created to minister to him and carry out his will and serve him and to minister to us. But lucifer didn't want to do that anymore, and God didn't allow it, so there was a battle in heaven and lucifer was thrown out of heaven along with a third of the angels who chose to follow him.

God doesn't share his glory with anybody and he would not allow his creation to take his glory. Here we are, made in God's image and here is lucifer, jealous of our position. God has given us so much power that we don't even understand what we have been given. He has given us so many gifts that make satan jealous of us.

When lucifer was cast out of heaven and sent down to earth, man was still in charge of the planet. This is the reason why, when he came to deceive Eve, he had to lie and manipulate her in order to get her to forfeit her power. Rather than be obedient to God's commands, she chose to submit her authority to somebody she was above spiritually. We sometimes submit our wills to satan and dance to his tunes and go along with whatever he wants to do, but he is beneath us.

Jesus Christ came to earth to strip satan of that authority, and now we are seated above him with Jesus Christ in heavenly places. We are not just sinners saved by grace, we are seated in heavenly places far above principalities and powers. If you read the book of Acts, Stephen saw Jesus seated at the right hand of God with his own eyes, and we are seated with Christ. Principalities and powers are the highest rank in the kingdom of darkness that rule with satan and we are FAR ABOVE them. If we don't know our place in God and who we are in him; if we don't understand what we carry, the enemy will mess us up because he's trying to hide the truth from us that we are completely loaded with the power and personality of the Father.

We were made in the image of the creator of the whole universe and not with precious stones. Genesis says we have the image of God and we are also adopted and graphed into the kingdom as sons and daughters.

There is a revelation that God gave me a long time ago. When the enemy tries to come and tell you that you're nobody and a loser or a failure, and that nobody loves you, he is lying and whenever he does that, I think about the revelation that satan should be ashamed of himself because he used to be in heaven enjoying life with the Father, but now he is living in hell and even a child has authority over him. If a five year old child is born again, he has more power than satan and all of his demons. This five year old has the authority to command satan to leave a person, and he must leave. Whenever I remind him of that, he runs because he knows it's the truth. We can't allow him to lie to us and believe that he is telling us the truth. We are not the failures, he is; because he's the one who left his first abode, which was heaven. The reason people go into depression is because of his lies.

God is not the creator of depression, but the lies of the enemy cause it by his telling us all kinds of lies designed to make us feel sorry for ourselves. Before we know it, we're having a pity party and depression comes in, because he tells us who we are when we should be telling him who he is. satan cannot change the fact that you are a son or daughter of the Most High

God. satan doesn't have any DNA because he's a bastard who doesn't have a father. We cannot allow him to intimidate us or take the ground that God has given us and placed into our hands. We will not allow the enemy to destroy us with his lies but we will believe the truth.

Jesus said, you will know the truth and it will make you free, and that is why satan tries to hide the truth from the church. That is why many churches don't believe in casting out demons or deliverance ministry, and when the read about it they skip over or ignore it because they want to believe a lie. Just because they don't believe it doesn't mean it's not true. That is why the enemy is destroying the people of God, because they lack knowledge. The bible says that the people perish because of a lack of knowledge. They lack the understanding of who they are and their position in Christ. It is by having the heart of the Father that we understand we have power and authority over the enemy. You don't' have to be a pastor, elder, bishop, deacon or even the pope to be above the enemy, but when you give your life to Jesus Christ you automatically become above the enemy. The truth that you get when you catch the revelation will open your eyes as to who you are, but if you don't understand that truth, you will always live beneath him. You are more than a conqueror through Christ Jesus. We are overcomers. We overcame satan by the blood of the lamb and the word of our testimony. The son of God is the LION, and he is always a LION!

Here is a prayer to pray:

Father, I thank you that you chose to create me in your own image and likeness and personality. Thank you that you chose to create me to look like you, and I know that I look like you because I came from you and have your DNA. I ask that you would open up my eyes to the spiritual realm, (Ephesians 1:18). I pray that any demonic activity against my life be broken, every ordinances and handwriting against me and my family I bring them under the subjection to the name of Jesus Christ. satan you are defeated and I am free. I close every entrance door and I take on the whole armor of God. I take on the mind of Jesus Christ, I silence every lie and any voices that are not from God. Jesus I yield and submit totally to your Lordship, in Jesus name Amen !

10

INHERITING NATIONS

"Giving thanks unto the Father, which hath made us meet to be partakers of the inheritance of the saints in light." *(Colossians 1:12)*

Inheritance wasn't a word used in our household.

We were taught to work for what we had, and that is how our life would go. Work, sleep, come home and eat dinner then do the same thing tomorrow. Any dreams that I had as a child and adolescent foreseeing future pieces of my destiny were silenced by work.

The time from 2008 to 2012 were darker years for us, filled with a period of testing and heartbreak. The call had to be tried and tested: Your greatest ministry always comes from your deepest pain.

"I will put them into the fire; I will refine them like silver and test them like gold. They will call on my name and I will answer them; I will say, 'They are my people,' and they will say, 'The LORD is our God.'" (Zechariah 13: 9 NIV)

One thing about receiving an inheritance is that you must know and believe that you actually have one. Every state has millions of dollars of unclaimed monies because the beneficiary simply did not know that they had anything owed to them. For example, if you were an estranged child of a wealthy man who passed away without your knowledge, and then years later, a lawyer contacted you to inform you of the inheritance; it would probably come as a total surprise to you. In the same way, children of the King who may be estranged from their Father's kingdom don't even realize that they have an inheritance awaiting them. It takes a true son or daughter who is in communication and has an intimate relationship with their Father to understand that everything that he has actually belongs to you as an heir to the kingdom.

As we see in the story of the prodigal son's older brother: His inheritance was based on intimacy. The Father told him "You're always with me so everything I have is already yours," (Luke 15:31) but the son never realized that he had access to the inheritance.

The only requirement to receive this inheritance is that you are saved and a son or daughter of the Kingdom. We are heirs to an inheritance because of one reason: Jesus Christ, who gave us access to the throne of grace through his shed blood on Calvary. We were slaves to our sin before Christ; we wouldn't control our sinful nature, it controlled us. This is a form of slavery and bondage. You tried everything in your power to cleanse yourself of sin, but you were unable to do so because it is a spiritual matter and not a matter of works or the flesh. We must allow ourselves to receive into our hearts the knowledge and belief that we are no longer slaves to sin but we are free to Christ. We are now heirs and heiresses to a kingdom greater than human hands, one designed and designated by a loving creator who died for us, so that we could share in this splendor.

"So you are no longer a slave, but God's child; and since you are his child, God has made you also an heir." (Galatians 4:7)

"Now if we are children, then we are heirs—heirs of God and co-heirs with Christ, if indeed we share in his sufferings in order that we may also share in his glory." (Romans 8:17)

How do we receive this gift? Like I stated earlier, it's a spiritual matter not a physical one, so the answer is spiritual even though it's very simple. We receive the spirit of adoption that allows us to call and know God as our Abba, Daddy. Adoption is a powerful thing and once it has been sealed, it can never be reversed. One cannot disown a child of adoption, as a matter of law. Adoption is a spiritual matter, and involves the changing of a position from orphan to son or daughter.

The Greek word for adoption (*huiothesia*) means to "place as a son." Another example would be a virgin espoused to her husband. On the wedding day she changes her status and position in life from bachelorette to wife. The major struggles we fight are changing our view or mindset that we are no longer slaves, but sons and daughters of God. This is where the spirit of adoption comes in and reminds us that we are children of the King. Joel and I travel all over parts of Africa and have encountered orphans whose parents have died prematurely due to AIDS or other circumstances. If we were to bring one of these children home, then apply for their U.S. Citizenship and then proceed with adoption hearings, they would become our children. Their placement would change physically, spiritually and naturally. But unless the spirit of adoption is present, they may struggle with receiving this special gift offered to them; especially if the child has experienced years of pain and neglect. The transition into a loving home could be a challenge for them and their mindset may remain in a state of believing they are unloved, even though that would be the farthest thing from the truth. I've met people who have a loving home life, and lack no material things, but refuse to go to that home and live in peace. They would rather sleep under a bridge with a needle in their arm instead of receiving the love waiting for them at home. This is a spiritual matter and no matter how hard we try in our own strength to change that mindset, it simply must be experienced by the person directly.

They must come to the realization and revelation that they are loved and accept and really believe it in their heart.

When the spirit of adoption is present there is an awareness on the inside of you that you are a true son or daughter of Christ. No circumstance can change the knowledge that you have deep inside that you belong to him. God's spirit whispers deep inside of you, assuring you that you're his child.

"The Spirit you received does not make you slaves, so that you live in fear again; rather, the Spirit you received brought about your adoption to sonship. And by him we cry, 'Abba, Father. The Spirit himself testifies with our spirit that we are God's children." (Romans 8:15, 16)

Once we grasp this revelation of truth, we can move forward with receiving our inheritance. Again, we can't receive our inheritance until we understand that we are an heir to the kingdom as a son or daughter. We can't show up at an estate executor's office and ask them to cut us an inheritance check from another person's father, unless we want the police called on us. We must be from the family or an heir to the inheritance in order to receive it from that lineage.

Prosperity preachers are predominately preaching passages from our pulpits in America on receiving an inheritance of money, wealth, riches, or substance. While all of this can be true, and prosperity teaching is important for those of us who have battled generational curses of poverty, they must never ever be the pinnacle of our message. Our message is Christ alone, and what he alone has done for us through his suffering, crucifixion, resurrection and promises for our future.

We have preached to tens of thousands of people on the mission field in Zimbabwe, Nigeria, the United Kingdom, Mali, and Cape Verde. While we have prayed and believed for this promise to come to pass during the past 10+ years, it is coming as a surprise and more revelation from our good Daddy and is teaching us new lessons and levels of trust in him. God began to give us the following verses on inheriting the nations of the world. This verse has been the highlight for this revelation:

"For the promise that he should be the heir of the world was not to Abraham and to his seed through the law but through righteousness of faith." (Romans 4:13)

God spoke to a fatherless man who was married to a barren woman at the ripe old age of 90 about a blessing or inheritance. He took Abraham into the Valley of Hebron one night and told him to "Look up at the stars in the sky." Then he goes on to tell him: "Look to the north, south, east and west. Do you see all those shining stars Abraham? Just look at them. Lift up your head, why are you looking down? I want to show you something. Something that you never even imagined could be possible Abraham. All you have to do is look up, imagine, and dream, and simply believe what I'm about to tell you. Do you see all of those stars in the sky? Well Abraham, as many of those stars as you can see, that is how many children you're going to have."

"What? Me? I'm 90. My wife is barren, and we've been trying to conceive a son for over fifty years, God. Respectfully sir, I believe you have the wrong man. My brother Lot would be a better choice God, don't you think? He has several children, four to be exact. You may be able to do something with his descendants, but I don't even have a son."

The "promise" given to Abraham is spoken of over 20 times in both the Old and New Testament, yet every commentary or study that I can find on the topic in America is about prosperity. Preachers in America who own three different million dollar houses, driving Bentley's, flying airplanes, and sporting thousand dollar shoes and suits are claiming that their wealth is the result of the "blessings of Abraham" which was promised to him by God in Genesis 12 and then passed down to us as descendants of Abraham and joint heirs with Jesus Christ. Houses, Cars, and Rolexes have replaced the blessings of God in our modern churches. The true blessing of God is our inheritance in Christ Jesus which is first of all, Salvation, and another facet of our inheritance is intended for the nations. When God gave Abraham this promise, he also told him that he would make him a "FATHER" of many nations. This is where the apostolic ministry comes into play. Apostolic ministry and global ministry work together hand in hand. True Apostles have the heart of a Father.

They desire to see their spiritual children thrive and do great things for our God. The apostolic and prophetic anointing is given for the sake of the nations.

When God spoke to Jeremiah, he told him "I have called you as a prophet to the nations." Basically, Jeremiah was to be God's mouthpiece, which comes with great responsibility including the building up of God's kingdom on earth and tearing down man's kingdoms. The prophets of old were given dreams and signs and wonders from God, many of which were specific instructions to kings and rulers of the earth, telling them that they should bow their knees to God. When these warnings were not adhered to, God's fury and wrath was poured out, not just on them, but their country as well, just as the prophets foretold.

The Apostle Paul planted churches all throughout Asia Minor and taught new believers in Christ to turn from their idols and worship the true and living God. This mandate is the same today as it was back then. Part of the great commission is discipling nations: teaching them everything that God has commanded us to do as believers. That means teaching people how to pray, worship, study the Bible, and live for Jesus Christ no matter the cost or circumstances. This works both ways, to and from America.

Here are some statistics on world missions:

- There are over 430,000 missionaries from all branches of Christendom. Of these, only between 2 and 3% of these missionaries work among unreached peoples. The other 98% work in Christian nations. (The Traveling Team)
- US based ministries send out over 144,000 short-term missionaries each year. Of these, only half of them last the entire way through their first term on the field.
- The average American Christian gives only 1 penny a day to global missions while Christian organizations spend $8 billion a year on conferences (Joshua Project)

These numbers are sobering, challenging, and compelling. We have the true gospel of Jesus Christ and it is our mandate to preach this gospel to all nations (Matthew 28).

Psalm 2:7-8, , Ask me, and I will make the nations your inheritance, the ends of the earth your possession."

The Father desires to give us the nations as our inheritance and the ends of the earth to possess. All we have to do is ask him. Why should we ask him? When we ask, we are exercising our faith and partnering with his purposes. We are setting our hearts in agreement with the promise and asking God to use us. Asking is an act of faith on our part and God always honors faith because it's the currency of heaven. God loved Abraham so much because he believed in him by faith. Abraham believed that God would make him the Father of many nations without his having one single child. That's the kind of radical, unreasonably, crazy kind of faith we can possess as descendants of Abraham and joint heirs with Jesus Christ.

"Blessed are the meek, for they will inherit the earth." (Matthew 5:5)

Meekness: An attitude of humble, submissive and expectant trust in God, and a loving, patient and gentle attitude towards others.

We inherit the earth and nations for one reason: so that we can act in humility and serve the nations as ambassadors of Jesus Christ. When Christ is revealed through our lives, people are changed and blessed through us. When individuals are changed, cities are changed, when cities are changed, nations are changed. God chooses to bless people through other people. I heard somebody say once that there aren't any Fed-Ex trucks making runs between heaven and earth. God chooses to use people to help people. We must not turn the other cheek to someone who is hungry or poor, especially in poverty-stricken nations.

Here in America, there are several if not hundreds of food banks and financial assistance agencies in every city. We don't have to travel very far to get a food box or a hot meal from our local mission. You can even pick up a food box for your pet nowadays. By contrast, there is only one large food bank organization in South Africa called FoodBank South Africa, and it didn't exist until 2009. In America over 46 million people per year are served at our local food banks, not to mention food Stamps. The USDA says there were 23,052,388 households on food stamps in 2013. That is over 23 million households' not individual recipients. Each household averages 3 members, so that translates to over 69 million Americans getting food stamps, yet we still have the audacity to claim there are hungry people in America.

America, we are only blessed by God so that we can be a blessing. Who are we to be a blessing to? God's heart is always for us to help the stranger, the orphan, the widow and the poor.

"Pure and genuine religion in the sight of God the Father means caring for orphans and widows in their distress and refusing to let the world corrupt you." (James 1:27 NLT)

The reason this covenant and inheritance is available to us is for the appropriation of the Kingdom of God to come to earth. We are to use the resources that we have to help the nations of the earth.

Inheriting nations was a covenant that God himself made with Abraham in Genesis 12:2-3. There was something in Abraham that God saw that caused Him to think this man was special: it was faith.

"Abraham believed God, and it was credited to him as righteousness." (Romans 4:3)

"Understand, then, that those who have faith are children of Abraham. Scripture foresaw that God would justify the Gentiles by faith, and announced the gospel in advance to Abraham: 'All nations will be blessed through you.' So those who rely on faith are blessed along with Abraham, the man of faith." (Galatians 3:7-9)

In Genesis 2:15, when God placed Adam in the garden, he told him to care for the earth. It was his inheritance and job as the son of our creator to multiply and to care for God's creation. We know that creation itself (earth and the other planets), cry out for the manifestation of the sons of God (Romans 8:19).

The earth speaks and has a voice. All of creation is speaking and singing the songs of God. Part of our inheritance is the earth (Matthew 5:5). We should be able to walk into a household, city, state, or nation and decree and declare the word of the Lord and the nations will bow. Joel 2:10 speaks about how a mighty army of believers will arise that will literally shake the earth. Nations will quake and shake at the power that this end time army carries and releases into the earth. All of the earth, including all of the nations will see his glory before Jesus returns to the earth. This glory will be seen all around the earth as we release his power and light through the gospel of Jesus Christ into the earth before the end of the age. The cosmos will experience the glory of God once again, as it did in the Garden of Eden.

"May all kings bow down to him and all nations serve him." (Psalm 72:11)

We live in a time when it's offensive to speak the name of Jesus, especially in non-Christian nations. Recently, when we were in Israel, I asked a military man who was guarding the entrance to the temple in Jerusalem where I could get in to access the temple for sightseeing purposes. He responded "There is no longer a temple here, only a mosque." The name of Jesus is above every other name, and the bible says that all kings will bow before and serve him. It's up to us to proclaim the message of the King in the nations of the world.

"I will shake all nations, and what is desired by all nations will come, and I will fill this house with glory,' says the LORD Almighty." (Haggai 2:7)

There is a shaking, unrest and underlying fear sweeping across the globe due to natural disasters, wars, famines and persecutions. Just this week our president addressed the nation, stating that the ISIS terrorist organization in Iraq had beheaded a pair of American journalists and Christian children. Christians are being be-headed and slaughtered in Nigeria by the dozens by muslim terrorists. It's time we wake up and stand in the face of evil and proclaim the love and good news of Jesus Christ and receive the inheritance we have been given. The nations do not belong to Al Qaeda, ISIS or any other terrorist organization but they belong to us because of Jesus Christ. The times that we are living in are desperate and very soon, proclaiming Christ in the nations will be against the law, and so we must act now. We need to activate our missionary troops and send them out to the far corners of the earth, proclaiming that Christ is King. If Americans are so reluctant to even give finances to world missions, than how can we expect them to put themselves in harm's way.

All of creation is longing, waiting, and yearning for his glory to be manifested throughout all the nations of the earth. In Matthew 28, the commission was given to us as believers to disciple nations. It's not up to the angels or the world, but it's up to you and me as heirs of God through Christ Jesus to see his kingdom released on the earth as it is in heaven. Even the rocks and mountains sing to God and cry out to him when there is no praise being brought forth on the earth, so there is a constant song being sung to heaven from earth (Luke 19:40).

"The Lord reigns; let the earth rejoice; Let the many islands be glad. Clouds and thick darkness surround Him; Righteousness and justice are the foundation of His throne. Fire goes before Him, And burns up His adversaries round about. His lightning's lit up the world; The earth saw and trembled. The mountains melted like wax at the presence of the Lord, At the presence of the Lord of the whole earth. The heavens declare His righteousness, And all the peoples have seen His glory." (Psalm 97:1-6)

"Worthy art Thou, our Lord and our God, to receive glory and honor and power; for Thou didst create all things, and because of Thy will they existed, and were created" (Revelation 4:11)

Valleys sing to him (Psalm 65:9-13) When he speaks, his voice is like water and he makes the lightning and wind from his storehouse. (Jeremiah 10:13)

We were born with a desire in our hearts for the will of God on earth, but those desires are killed by media, violence, sex, drugs and the like. It's only when we receive our spiritual inheritance in Christ that his heart's desires become our desires and we long to see his kingdom manifested on earth just as it is in heaven. Jesus is the desire of the nations. Every person on earth has a deep longing inside of them to know their creator. If you were placed in solitary confinement for an entire year with no television or internet and the only communication you had was the inner voice inside of you, your idea of "life" would definitely change.

Everyday life creates a great deal of clutter in our heads which tunes out the desire for God inside of us. We are taught to get up every day, shower, eat, go to work, run errands, eat dinner and then repeat it all over again the next day. We do this until we retire at 65 and then we wonder why we have no substance or relationship with Christ in our lives. Desperate times call for desperate measures, and we must awaken our spiritual senses to the realization that Jesus Christ is Lord, and not just Lord over our little neck of the woods, but over the entire earth. The earth is a really big place and there are hundreds of different tribes, tongues and groups of people on planet earth. Unless you've travelled extensively internationally and visited poor and dying orphans and villages, you might not ever know that firsthand. Sure, we watch 30 minute specials on children starving in Africa and become moved to tears, but then we change the channel when it gets to be a little bit too much for us to handle and quickly forget about what we had just seen. The reality is that every day over 100,000 people die without ever knowing Jesus Christ as Lord, and that needs to change.

This longing and desire in our hearts was placed there by God, and it's a mystery that we don't understand but the wisest man that ever walked the planet, Solomon, said it like this:

"He has made everything beautiful in its time. He has also set eternity in the human heart; yet no one can fathom what God has done from beginning to end." (Ecclesiastes 3:11)

God is summoning the nations with his splendor. We know that where sin abounds, the grace of God abounds even greater. While we are surrounded by human atrocities such as abortion, war, famine and terrorism, we know that God will still have his way with his people on the earth. In these latter times his spirit is drawing those who are called by his name to himself. My prayer is that we answer that call, surrender our hearts in love to him as an offering of fire on the altar.

"Surely you will summon nations you know not, and nations you do not know will come running to you, because of the LORD your God, the Holy One of Israel, for he has endowed you with splendor."
ISAIAH 55:5

.

CPSIA information can be obtained
at www.ICGtesting.com
Printed in the USA
FSOW03n1235280218
45139FS

9 780578 160511